THE

surrender

PRAYER

*Where We
End and God
Begins*

KRISTIAN LYNCH, LCSW

Printed in the United States of America

First Printing, 2017

ISBN 978-0-9989411-0-3

Cover and interior design by Emily Weigel
Cover image © Stocksy

Surrendered Publishing
4 South Orange Avenue
No. 278
South Orange, NJ 07079

www.TheSurrenderPrayer.com

With the most profound thanks, I wish to dedicate this book to:

my clients who have challenged me and taught me far more than any school, church, teacher or "expert" in the helping professions;

Ed Lyons, my mentor and "brotha' from anotha' motha'";

Naomi, Zoe and Layla, my daughters "who keep me human"; and

Berny, my wife, partner, greatest friend, confidante, mother of my children, and light of my life down here on this earth.

CONTENTS

PREFACE

As a licensed clinical social worker, I've worked with people from every part of our society. The rich and the poor. The homeless. The unemployed. People with college degrees and those without. Black, White, Asian, Latino, and multi-racial clients. The old and the young. The healthy and the infirm. Male, female, straight, gay, lesbian, bisexual, queer, and questioning. The addicted and the abused, those who were neglected or traumatized. The depressed, anxious, and bi-polar. Christians, Muslims, Buddhists, atheists, and agnostics…and many more. I've learned, however, that the labels we assign to differentiate each other are meaningless. We are all children of God. We all struggle. We all experience some level of pain, and we all desperately need God. This book represents my search for a solution to the pain, suffering, and addictions that both my clients and I have experienced in life.

The Surrender Prayer is intended for those of us who have reached the end of our ropes: those of us who have been forced to accept that we cannot make it on our own. We have been searching for a path to overcome the hurt, suffering, temptations, sin, cravings, or addictions that have saddled us. We have been searching for an explanation for our pain, but also for a means to triumph over it.

I wrote this guide for those of us who can no longer deny our weakness, wounds, oppression and brokenness—for those of us who have accepted (some more readily than others) that we are utterly dependent upon the power of God to attain a freedom from the pain of this world and from ourselves.

God does not view weakness and strength the way that the world views it. For God, our admission of powerlessness and our awareness, acceptance, and increasing dependence upon God are the first steps to strength. Our denial of our God need is true weakness—our confession of this need is the starting point of true strength.

The message of this book is not one that is preached on Sundays in the vast majority of America's churches. It is a sobering message. It is a message rooted in the whole of reality—a message that is reflected clearly in the life and teachings of Jesus Christ. But it is also a message that exposes the shortcomings of what is found so often in much of Christian "religion."

Throughout my life, I have asked God endless times to free me from my sins, temptations, addictions, and hurts. I have searched everywhere for a way to escape the struggles and disappointments of my life. I have examined the suffering that visits the oppressed, the abused, the poor, and the powerless in this world. And I have demanded an explanation from God for the pain that is an inevitable fact of life. The wounded part of me that cries out to God daily—and has cursed God periodically—questions his sovereignty, his very existence, his benevolence, and his love. How could this part of me not ask such questions?

These thoughts, however, make me no less of a Christian. After all, if Jesus questioned his Father on the cross—why wouldn't we? These issues confirm at the most basic level what the walk of a Christian is: to somehow find God through all the questions, doubts, fears, anger, sadness, hurt, frustration, and injustice. Our purpose is to find God through the pain. To somehow learn to reach his love in this world when, at times, so little of it appears to exist.

I am a believer. My life experiences have confirmed that my God does exist. I cannot deny what he has done for me and for others. Nor can I deny all of the evil and pain that he allows to exist and thrive in this world.

God allows the most horrendous evil to touch the most innocent. God does not always "show up" and save the day in the way that I hoped or expected he would when I was younger. God often allows evil to prosper to the apparent detriment of that which is good. Being a Christian fails to support the common refrain that God does not give us more than we can bear—evidence to the contrary abounds. I believe the opposite to be true. God purposely allows us to experience far more than we are capable of enduring for one very important purpose: for us to cry out to him and to receive him in our need just as his Son did on the cross.

God's love is somehow connected with the pain and suffering that he allows. My faith necessitates this conclusion because allowing suffering without a loving purpose would make God sadistic or at the very least uncaring or powerless. What saves me from these inevitable conclusions is the path that Jesus took to the cross.

We know that Jesus suffered on the cross, and we believe that Jesus was God "made flesh" (John 1:14). These two premises support the conclusion that we serve a suffering God: a God that consented to suffering in order to redeem all of humanity and to show us a clear path to himself. God allowed Jesus to be crucified on the cross—even after Jesus asked his Father to take "this cup" from him. Therefore, why should we believe that God would (or should) offer us a way to escape the suffering and pain of the world when he refused to save himself (Jesus) from that same suffering and pain?

Understanding Jesus's prayer in the Garden of Gethsemane (where Jesus had to be strengthened by God before proceeding to the cross) is a key to understanding the Surrender Prayer described in this book. The Surrender Prayer does not provide an escape from pain, suffering, and temptation. It enables you to access the power of the Holy Spirit so that you can: persevere and overcome the trials of life, receive God's spiritual blessings, begin living your life to the fullest, and ultimately fulfill the purpose for which you were created (John 10:10).

We practice the Surrender Prayer to access God and his unconditional love for us. The prayer's application is not limited to assisting you to work through your spiritual and emotional wounds: its practice has many other uses as well. While the purpose of this short book will be limited to discovering how this prayer can be used as a means to help you manage and heal your pain, the daily practice of the Surrender Prayer will, over time, also help you:

- feel God's presence,
- rest in God's presence,
- hear God's voice,
- develop greater patience,
- gain greater self-awareness and insight,
- resist temptation,
- strengthen and improve your relationship with God,
- discover more of who God is, and
- experience God's unconditional love and acceptance.

The start of your Surrender Prayer practice marks the beginning of a new journey to draw closer to your God. And as you progress in this practice, you will find God by your side every step of the way.

SAFETY

It is extremely important that we are prodigiously kind and patient with ourselves during all steps of the Surrender Prayer. Safety comes first and should always come first. We only confront and bring into the light of God's healing love those issues, feelings, thoughts, and memories that we can do so safely. If there is any chance—no matter how remote—that confronting a particular issue will lead to panic attacks, depression, suicidal ideation, disassociation, suicide attempts, flashbacks, or any other dangerous consequence, we do not utilize this prayer.

We should learn to trust ourselves to know when enough is enough. While we pray, if we ever feel overwhelmed or unsafe for any reason, we simply open our eyes and end the prayer.

In addition, if you are currently receiving (or have ever received) psychiatric care, psychotropic medication, or psychotherapy for any mental health issue, please consult with a psychiatrist or other licensed mental health professional before beginning to practice the Surrender Prayer.

Feeling unsafe, however, is not the same as feeling uncomfortable. Feeling unsafe during this Prayer is to be avoided at all costs, but feeling discomfort is to be expected and should at some point be accepted if we desire true change. You may experience anxiety, worry, fear, sadness, anger, disgust, shame, and many other emotions, but these feelings are OK to feel as long as they are safe to feel. This prayer requires you to confront those aspects of yourself that you have been purposely avoiding in various ways for years—so you will, of course, experience some level of discomfort. Nevertheless, when you confront your inner struggles, please remember that: (1) you are the ultimate arbiter in deciding how far to safely push yourself; and (2) you should always err on the side of caution.

INTRODUCTION

> *Then they cried to the Lord in their trouble, and he*
> *saved them from their distress. He sent out his word*
> *and healed them; he rescued them from the grave.*
> *Let them give thanks to the Lord for his unfailing*
> *love and his wonderful deeds for mankind.*
>
> **Psalm 107:19–21 (NIV)**

The Surrender Prayer has grown from my personal journey to fill the gaps that characterize both traditional psychotherapy and the majority of mainline Christian churches. For me, psychotherapy that does not help clients access the healing power of the Holy Spirit is, at best, incomplete. And Christianity that does not reveal the unconditional acceptance, encouragement, empathy, kindness, support, accountability, healthy confrontation, partnership, honesty, authenticity, patience, forgiveness, non-judgmental stance, safety, and trust of effective psychotherapy is a mockery of the message of our Lord and Savior, Jesus Christ.

There exists an unfortunate rift between the religion that is taught in far too many of today's churches, and the secular psychotherapy approaches that do not include Christian spirituality as any part of their treatment paradigm. As a consequence, many people in pain give up on God, and turn to psychotherapy as their new religion. When this shift occurs, the therapist commonly becomes the substitute priest or minister to whom the client confesses his or her sins and struggles. The danger inherent in such relationships is the very real possibility that the client becomes more dependent upon their therapist than he or she is upon God—just as many Christians are far more dependent upon ministers, televangelists, conferences, retreats, and denominations than they are on God.

Alternatively, hurting Christian believers, who need more mental health resources than their local churches can provide, are often prevented from accessing such support because of the ignorance, fear, and intolerance of much present-day, mainline, Christian religion. Some level of stigma or shame commonly attaches to any believers who require more help than what their churches have to offer. Consequently, many Christians never venture outside of the confines of their local church community to receive the help they desperately need.

The Surrender Prayer is one approach to bridge the gap between effective psychotherapy and the church. The presumed dichotomy between the two is false: effective psychotherapy techniques at their core reflect the empathic understanding, genuineness, and unconditional love and acceptance of Jesus Christ; and effective Christianity enables believers to access the power of the Holy Spirit to tear down any stronghold. The Surrender Prayer presents an effective integration of both.

What you have in your hands is not a self-help book. The Surrender Prayer does not offer a futile fifty-word formula for you to bend the will of God to match your own—that doesn't work. The Surrender Prayer is not a mantra or a prayer of vain repetitions. The Surrender Prayer does not align with the mistaken religious belief that it is God's will to bless all Christians with financial rewards and physical well-being. And The Surrender Prayer does not offer you an easy path to recovery and healing. You will find no shortcuts, gimmicks, or empty promises here. The benefits you receive from the Surrender Prayer depend upon how willing you are to begin trusting and surrendering your fears, defenses, and will to a loving God.

three steps

The Surrender Prayer was created specifically as a daily prayer practice to enlist the power of God to aid you in your suffering and struggles. The Surrender Prayer presents a three-step prayer of Awareness, Acceptance, and Surrender that you will pray in your own words.

The Awareness step will require you to look deeply into yourself and begin the process of discovering the origins of your struggles. This step will help you examine the hurtful feelings, thoughts, experiences, and current circumstances that lead to self-destructive behaviors, sin, addiction, anxiety, depression, and low self-esteem. The first step is not a fun step, but it is a very necessary one. It is impossible to begin the work of solving a problem until you become aware of both its existence and its cause.

The second step is Acceptance. This step will teach you how to stop disassociating from and rejecting who you are, what you've done, and all that's been done to you. The Acceptance step is about learning how to let the light of God's love shine down into dark, painful places so that you can begin accepting and loving yourself the way that God unconditionally accepts and loves you.

The third step is Surrender. This step will help you "let go, and let God." When we are finally able to recognize and accept the fact that we do not have the power or strength to successfully fight our own battles, we can begin the process of surrendering our battle to God so that he can begin fighting for us.

There is nothing magical about the Surrender Prayer. In fact, the Prayer's three components (Awareness, Acceptance, and Surrender) are derived directly from the Bible, as we will explore in the chapters to come.

The entire prayer itself can be completed in as little as fifteen minutes in the morning, afternoon, or night. I practice the Surrender Prayer everyday to help me fight my battles. In addition, I apply the tools and concepts presented herein to assist the amazing individuals that I counsel in my practice as a Christian psychotherapist.

The Surrender Prayer should be practiced daily in order to receive its full benefits. The Prayer in its entirety is presented on pages 191 (Summary Guide) and 193 (Full Instructions). You may also download a guided audio version of the prayer at www.TheSurrenderPrayer.com. The audio version of the prayer was designed as an optional, introductory support to jumpstart your Surrender Prayer practice. Please download it, and listen to all of it at least once to get a feel for what the Surrender Prayer is before actually beginning to use it as a guide.

As soon as you begin practicing the Surrender Prayer, you should commit to working through this book. Each chapter is designed to help you fully comprehend the purpose of each step so that you may successfully practice all three portions of the Prayer. If you fail to work through this book in its entirety, you will limit your understanding of the Surrender Prayer, and may hinder the effectiveness of your practice.

Each chapter, beginning with "Choosing a New Way," contains questions to help you dig deeper into yourself and into your relationship with God. These questions are included to help you unlock the issues that have prevented you from moving forward in your life.

Please do not skip or rush over the questions. It is extremely important that you answer each question to the best of your ability before moving on to the next chapter—you will shortchange yourself if you do not. In addition, starting in this chapter, you will find a closing prayer at the end of every chapter in this book. The closing prayer will help you assimilate and solidify the content of what you have just read and prepare you for what is to come next.

I purposely have not provided you with a set timetable to complete this book. If you commit to the Surrender Prayer, you will encounter and engage the most personal and delicate parts of yourself. Accordingly, you should ask for the Holy Spirit's direction as you progress. So please proceed at your own safe pace as you feel guided to do so. In other words, stop when you feel led to stop, and pick it up again as you feel led to return to the book. Above all, please be kind and patient with yourself as you move forward.

closing prayer

Dear God, please prepare me for the journey that you and I are about to take together. Open my mind, soul, spirit, and heart so that you and I may grow closer. Give me the strength, faith, and courage to dig deeper and begin the process of unraveling all that has blocked my freedom and healing. Guide me and keep me safe. Show me that you love me. And teach me how to be patient and loving with myself as we walk this path side-by-side. Amen.

CHOOSING A
NEW WAY

> *The weapons we fight with are not the weapons of the world. On the contrary, they have divine power to demolish strongholds.*
>
> **2 Corinthians 10:4 (NIV)**

The Surrender Prayer is a daily practice to help you improve your personal relationship with God. Its purpose is to clear away everything that hinders your connection to our Creator. We can practice the Prayer when we are happy, depressed, anxious, or facing a trigger that pushes us to act out in an unhealthy or sinful way. In short, our prayer practice is not dictated by our emotional state—but upon our belief that we need to maintain a secure connection to our higher power everyday.

* **Describe your current practice of prayer, Bible reading, and quiet time:**

_____

_____

_____

_____

_____

_____

_____

_____

The Surrender Prayer is a daily prayer that we can use to enlist God to join our battle against our own personal demons. If you are fortunate, you have experienced the beauty of life, but if you are reading this book, you have also been exposed to much of what makes this world an ugly place. Jesus taught us to resist our temptations and struggles by relying upon the power of God—not by relying upon our own willpower, intellect, or other personal resources. Our Prayer is about harnessing the power of God in a manner that allows him to fight our battles for us. The Surrender Prayer will only work for you if you have genuinely given up trying to do it your own way, and have no other choice but to try it God's way.

* **Describe your present spiritual condition. How close do you feel to God? Is God an active, positive, or helpful participant in your life?**

_____

_____

_____

_____

_____

_____

When we practice the Surrender Prayer, we strengthen our connection to the Creator, and we exercise our free will by giving our consent to the Holy Spirit to begin the process of healing our emotional and spiritual wounds. We consent to the Spirit's work in us by letting go and letting God do the work that we have admitted we cannot do for ourselves. While I believe that it is only natural to ask God to take away our "thorns of the flesh," this Prayer exists for those of us who may never be able to relinquish their cups to God. In other words, the Surrender Prayer was created to help us attain victory, one day at a time, over the struggles, temptations, and sins that we may potentially have to battle for the rest of our lives.

The Prayer is focused on enabling each of us to access a divine resource that will empower us to break the destructive strongholds within our lives. We believe unequivocally that Jesus won the ultimate war 2000 years ago, but his victory did not release us from our responsibility to pick up and carry our cross daily. The Surrender Prayer takes seriously Jesus' promise to make our yoke easier and burden lighter:

> *"Come to me, all you who are weary and burdened, and I will give you rest. Take my yoke upon you and learn from me, for I am gentle and humble in heart, and you will find rest for your souls. For my yoke is easy and my burden is light."*
> **Matthew 11:28–30 (NIV)**

As an alternative to choosing to continue down the path of our go-to quick fixes, which allow us a dysfunctional and temporary escape from pain, the Surrender Prayer forces us to confront the daily battle that is our life. Our go-to quick fixes are the survival skills and coping mechanisms that we employ to manage and endure our reality to the best of our abilities. These include: obsessive compulsions and addictions linked to alcohol, drugs, sex, depression, control, anger, gambling, perfectionism, work, exercise, video games, the Internet, religion, power, fame, celebrity, wealth, competition, love, relationships, guilt, people-pleasing, pornography, selfishness, racism, sexism, violence—virtually anything.

* What are your go-to quick fixes? What unhealthy behaviors, feelings, obsessions, thoughts, addictions, or compulsions do you use to distract yourself (or escape) from your struggles, problems, issues, fears, sadness, anger, boredom, loneliness, jealousy, weakness or pain?

_____

_____

_____

_____

_____

_____

_____

* When life gets too hard, how do you escape from reality? How do you live in denial of the true circumstances and conditions of your life?

_____

_____

_____

_____

_____

_____

* **Until now, how have you reacted to loss, pain, suffering or disappointment?**

_____

_____

_____

_____

_____

_____

* **As a child, what coping skills did you use to get attention or to protect yourself?**

_____

_____

_____

_____

_____

The Prayer is a means to help us come to grips with the fact that our go-to quick fixes and escapes no longer work—or at least no longer work as well as they once did. Whatever ephemeral satisfaction, if any, we received in the past from our distractions and numbing agents has become increasingly out-weighed by our awareness of the destructive consequences that it requires for its maintenance.

* **What have been the destructive consequences of continuing to use your go-to quick fixes and escapes? List the major ways that you have harmed yourself.**

_____

_____

_____

_____

_____

_____

* **How have your struggles caused injury to other people?**

_____

_____

_____

_____

_____

_____

It is time to begin the process of ridding ourselves of such self-destructive habits and to begin living a life of freedom in Christ. The following chapters will describe how the three steps of Awareness, Acceptance, and Surrender can help you enlist the power of the Holy Spirit to demolish negative strongholds in your life.

closing prayer

Dear God, please provide me with the spiritual resources that I need to begin fighting my battles with your divine weapons—not my worldly ones. Teach me how to let go of the self-destructive tools that I have used to endure my personal struggles. Show me how to enlist your help in my daily battles. Instruct me to use your weapons to tear down the strongholds in my life. And please allow me to discover what victory in Jesus means. Amen!

chapter 1

IDENTIFYING THE PAIN OF OUR PAST AND PRESENT

> *Let us examine our ways and test them, and let us return to the LORD.*
>
> **Lamentations 3:40 (NIV)**

The Awareness step of the Surrender Prayer will help you develop greater personal insight by examining what you've done, what you've been through, and what negative effects have resulted as a consequence of your life experiences. The Surrender Prayer enables us to cultivate our interior, spiritual life by directly promoting greater self-awareness. This awareness necessitates a level of stillness that may make many of us feel uncomfortable. To be still with our thoughts, feelings, and memories without distraction (or some other escape hatch) is to learn how to come face-to-face with all that we feel and think without running away. In this process, we put on the table all that pains us, shames us, scares us, embarrasses us, or saddens us; and we learn to look at it without turning from it. In time, we may learn to embrace all of it; but for now, we only need to bring such matters into focus.

* **What are your greatest fears? Please list those fears that have wielded the most negative power over your life since childhood.**

_____

_____

_____

_____

_____

_____

* **How do these fears currently affect your life?**

_____

_____

_____

_____

_____

* **What problems, memories, or wounds cause you the greatest sadness? Who or what depresses you?**

_____

_____

_____

_____

_____

_____

_____

* **What effect does such sadness have on your life?**

_____

_____

_____

_____

_____

* **Who or what causes you to experience unhealthy levels of anger? Explain.**

_____

_____

_____

_____

_____

* **What causes you unhealthy levels of anxiety? What do you always worry about? Why?**

_____

_____

_____

_____

_____

_____

As we grow in our Surrender Prayer practice, we learn to sit with and face our "junk." We learn that we can think what we think, remember what we remember, and feel what we feel without resorting to our destructive compulsions, behaviors, and addictions. Awareness dictates that we become increasingly aware of who and what we are in Christ:

> *See what great love the Father has lavished on us, that we should be called children of God! And that is what we are!*
>
> **1 John 3:1 (NIV)**

* **Are there unresolved issues from your past that you fear remembering or revisiting? If so, please describe.**

_____

_____

_____

_____

_____

_____

* **What wrongs have you committed that keep you awake at night?**

_____

_____

_____

_____

_____

* **What wrongs have you endured (or survived) that keep you awake at night?**

_____

_____

_____

_____

_____

* **What resentments do you have against others that keep you awake at night?**

_____

_____

_____

_____

_____

_____

* **What secret sins keep you awake at night?**

_____

_____

_____

_____

_____

_____

* **What are the greatest losses that you have experienced in life? Are you
still grieving these losses? Why?**

_____

_____

_____

_____

_____

Taking the Awareness step of the Surrender Prayer helps us break through
our fears, denial, pride, shame, prejudice, and other emotional and cognitive
barriers that prevent us from discovering the fundamental truth of ourselves:
that we are in desperate need of a loving God to heal us!

The more we deny and run away from who we are, the more we remain the
same. We can stop running from who we are, what we've done, and what's
been done to us. But we cannot change the behaviors, emotions, and thoughts
that entangle us until we come face-to-face with them and understand the
psychology that gives rise to such behaviors, emotions, and thoughts. If we

continue denying all that we are, we will never be able to decipher the underlying causes of the unhealthy or sinful behaviors that separate us from the unconditional love of God. If we continue to deny all that we are, we prevent the light of God's unconditional love from illuminating and healing the dark places of our souls.

* **Since childhood, what have been your most painful life experiences?**

_____

_____

_____

_____

_____

_____

* **What harmful thoughts or feelings about yourself (or others) have resulted from these experiences?**

_____

_____

_____

_____

_____

The Awareness step will increase your level of self-awareness by quieting the distractions around you so that you can recognize and face your pain, denial, unhealthy behaviors, destructive patterns, weaknesses, and internal conflicts. Each time you practice awareness, you confront the issues that you have identified as causing your day-to-day physical, mental, emotional, or spiritual battles.

* **Who or what has hurt you most in your life (please go as far back as you can)? How did they specifically hurt you?**

_____

_____

_____

_____

_____

* **How does what happened still affect you today?**

_____

_____

_____

_____

* **In which current relationship do you feel the most guilt or shame? Please explain.**

_____

_____

_____

_____

_____

* **Which of your current relationships cause you the most pain in terms of unforgiveness and resentment? Toward whom are you bitter, resentful or angry? Why?**

_____

_____

_____

_____

_____

_____

* **Whom are you emotionally or otherwise unwilling or unable to forgive? Why?**

_____

_____

_____

_____

_____

_____

* **Does this inability to forgive interfere with your relationship with God?**

_____

_____

_____

_____

_____

* **Does it interfere with your own personal joy and progress? Has your inability to forgive caused you problems or other issues?**

_____

_____

_____

_____

_____

* **In what ways do you feel powerless or weak in dealing with these relationships?**

_____

_____

_____

_____

_____

* How have you sought to control or manipulate others to fulfill your own needs and wants?

_____

_____

_____

_____

_____

* Whom have you seriously harmed? In what ways have you hurt them (e.g., professionally, sexually, educationally, morally, financially, spiritually, emotionally, socially, physically, verbally, or mentally)? Do you still hurt them?

_____

_____

_____

_____

_____

_____

* Why?

_____

_____

_____

_____

_____

Each time we practice awareness in the Surrender Prayer, we will be required to: (1) bring our specific struggles out into the open, and (2) present them to our loving God. We will intentionally drag into God's loving light those aspects of ourselves that we attempt to hide from ourselves, from others, and from God. We do our best to place ourselves unguarded before him, and seek to find a place where pretense, shame, guilt and embarrassment no longer prevent us from being authentic in his presence.

closing prayer

Dear God, please give me the faith, strength, and courage to look deep inside myself. Please open my eyes so that I can clearly see how the pain and struggles of my life have blocked me from receiving your unconditional love. Amen!

chapter 2

A RETURN TO THE GARDEN OF EDEN

In a sense, the first step of the Prayer is a figurative return to the Garden of Eden. We are seeking a place where we can be unclothed before God like Adam and Eve once were, but without the shame that overwhelmed them when they sinned. One of the greatest misconceptions that many Christians share is that we cannot approach God with our weakness and sin. We somehow believe that our failures compel God to reject us. This belief couldn't be further from the truth. God didn't hide from Adam and Eve when they sinned: it was God that went looking for them after they both ate the apple. We were the ones that attempted to hide, and we continue to hide from him to this day.

Consequently, the first step of the Prayer is to stop hiding. God did not clothe Adam and Eve in the garden because of what they did with the apple. That is, God did not cover us because he couldn't stand to look at us uncovered after we sinned. God clothed Adam and Eve in the garden because we (humankind) could no longer look at God the same way after we sinned. He clothed us because we could no longer stand before him unclothed. In other words, God's view or opinion of us didn't change, our opinion and view of God changed! We did not see him as someone who could love us through our failures. Instead, we came to see him as someone who would reject and punish us for our failures.

* **Since childhood, what have been your most painful failures?**

_____

_____

_____

_____

_____

_____

_____

* **List those experiences when you've felt most rejected by people.**

_____

_____

_____

_____

_____

_____

* **Have you ever felt rejected by God? When?**

_____

_____

_____

_____

_____

_____

_____

* **What's so scary about being completely honest with God about who you are, what you've done, what you think, and what you feel? Why is it scary?**

_____

_____

_____

_____

_____

_____

As stated previously, this guide's application of the Prayer is for those of us who struggle with past hurts, addictions, harmful obsessions and compulsions, and unhealthy feelings of guilt, sadness, anxiety or low self-esteem. We use the Prayer to invite God into our pain so that God can begin healing those parts of us that have been left unhealed.

We will learn that we can bring anything to God. We need to believe that our God is not ashamed of us, that he will never reject us, and that he loves us with a love that we could never comprehend. So whatever you have locked inside of yourself that causes you shame, fear, guilt or embarrassment, please understand that God does not see you the way that you see yourself—or the way that we believe others see us. Not only has our God already forgiven <u>all</u> of our sins, failures, and weaknesses, he has also <u>forgotten</u> all of our sins, failures, and weaknesses:

> *"This is the covenant I will establish with the people of Israel after that time, declares the Lord. I will put my laws in their minds and write them on their hearts. I will be their God, and they will be my people. No longer will they teach their neighbors, or say to one another, 'Know the Lord,' because they will all know me, from the least of them to the greatest. For I will forgive their wickedness and will remember their sins no more."*
>
> **Hebrews 8:10–12 (*NIV*)**

* **In what areas do you doubt God's ability to forgive you and release you from all of your sins or struggles?**

_____

_____

_____

_____

_____

_____

_____

This is your opportunity to unload your baggage. This is your chance to throw off everything that hinders you and all the sin that so easily entangles:

> *Therefore, since we are surrounded by such a great cloud of witnesses, let us throw off everything that hinders and the sin that so easily entangles. And let us run with perseverance the race marked out for us, fixing our eyes on Jesus, the pioneer and perfecter of faith. For the joy that was set before him he endured the cross, scorning its shame, and sat down at the right hand of the throne of God. Consider him who endured such opposition from sinners, so that you will not grow weary and lose heart.*
>
> **Hebrews 12:1–3 (*NIV*)**

Begin the process of laying your burdens down—and realize that God never intended for you to carry such a heavy load. If Jesus said: "Come to me, all of you who are weary and carry heavy burdens, and I will give you rest" (Matthew 11:28)—what are you waiting for?

closing prayer

Dear God, I don't want to be afraid of you anymore. I don't want to be ashamed or embarrassed when I come into your presence. Please give me the faith to believe that all of my sins have been forgiven, and that I don't have to hide from you. Help me believe that you've never rejected me and that you never will. Please establish our relationship anew in love—not fear. Amen!

chapter 3

PICKING YOUR BATTLES

The Awareness step requires us to pick and choose our battles. We identify and select a specific problem or issue that we are battling (for example: poverty, illness, oppression, toxic emotions, a harmful addiction, temptation or sin) as the struggle we wish to present to God. The struggle you identify and select will stem from your own wounds or problems. The struggle you select may make you feel ugly, unworthy, broken, weak, less than, guilty, irredeemable, or anxious.

You need only identify one personal struggle at a time when you practice the Prayer. But the struggle that you initially choose will most likely be the particular problem or issue that drew you to begin learning about the Surrender Prayer in the first place.

* **Make a list of all your self-destructive and self-defeating behaviors, thoughts, and feelings.**

_____

_____

_____

_____

_____

_____

_____

_____

* **Which of these behaviors, thoughts, and feelings are most damaging to your life and to others you care about?**

_____

_____

_____

_____

_____

_____

* **What have been the consequences of these behaviors, thoughts, and feelings?**

_____

_____

_____

_____

_____

_____

* **Why do you believe you still continue to struggle with these behaviors, thoughts, and feelings?**

_____

_____

_____

_____

_____

When our struggle is causing us distress, we will utilize the Surrender Prayer to address the problem that is causing us pain in the present moment. But there may be occasions when we have difficulty identifying the exact nature of what is currently troubling us. If we find ourselves in this situation, we simply ask the Holy Spirit to help us identify the problem or issue that God wants us to treat as the identified struggle for the Prayer.

* **Ask God to reveal to you the issues that he would like you to begin working on. These are issues that we may not yet currently be conscious or aware of. Please pray for a few minutes and then list those areas below.**

_____

_____

_____

_____

_____

Please remember that we only bring to God those struggles that we can safely bring before God when we are alone with him. If there is any question or doubt in your mind about the safety of confronting a particular wound or problem during the Prayer, please do not confront such a matter until after you have first consulted with a licensed mental health professional. For example, individuals who suffer from PTSD, panic attacks, suicidal ideation, or schizophrenia should first consult with a licensed mental health professional before practicing any portion of the Prayer.

We do not select struggles that have been successfully healed or resolved for the Prayer. The purpose of the Awareness step is not to rehash resolved issues. We only bring to God those struggles that currently cause us clear and present harm, or distress in our daily lives.

For example:
- An alcoholic may bring his addiction to alcohol or his craving for a drink to God.
- A drug addict may bring her addiction to opiates or her craving for heroin to God.
- A widow may bring her unresolved grief over the death of her husband to God.
- A divorcee may bring the guilt that he feels over abandoning or neglecting his ex-wife and children to God.
- A mother may bring the guilt she feels over losing her children to a state's child protective services agency to God.
- A married woman may bring her desire to have an affair with a coworker to God.

Additionally:
- A sex addict may bring his addiction to pornography, strip clubs, prostitutes, masturbation, or pornography to God.
- A woman may bring the unhealed pain of a prior abortion to God.
- An impoverished, single mother may bring the distress that she feels about being on welfare to God.

- A Native American may bring the anguish he feels about being part of an oppressed minority to God.
- A Christian may bring her frustration about all the injustice, oppression, and evil that are allowed to flourish in this world to God.
- An adolescent may bring the confusion and despair that he feels about his sexual orientation to God.

And furthermore:
- An abused wife may bring the pain of feeling trapped in a domestically violent relationship to God.
- An unmarried, middle-aged woman may bring the pain she feels about feeling lonely, unwanted, and unloved to God.
- A married man may bring the pain that he feels about the desperate state of his marriage to God.
- A mother may bring the fear and helplessness she feels about one of her children being addicted to prescription painkillers to God.
- And, lastly, a Christian may bring his anger at God for all the pain he has suffered in his lifetime to God.

What we bring to God is anything that we have identified as causing us pain and distress. What we bring to God is the struggle that we believe will or already has separated us from the healing power of God's unconditional, unlimited, and all-powerful love. What we bring to God is our confession: our acknowledgement and admission of some personal struggle that we usually keep hidden from ourselves, from others, and from God.

* **What burden weighs heaviest on your heart?**

_____

_____

_____

_____

_____

_____

_____

* **What struggles do you believe prevent you from drawing closer to God?**

_____

_____

_____

_____

_____

The Prayer's first step of Awareness demands that we confess our struggles with sin, weakness and powerlessness. In other words, this Awareness step requires us to acknowledge and to proclaim (to our self and to our God) the daily struggles that only the power of God can help us endure, heal, forgive, repair or manage.

> _If we say that we have no sin, we are only fooling our-selves and refusing to accept the truth. But if we confess our sins to him, he can be depended on to forgive us and to cleanse us from every wrong. And it is perfectly proper for God to do this for us because Christ died to wash away our sins._
>
> **1 John 1:8–9 (_TLB_)**

Whoever conceals their sins does not prosper, but the one who confesses and renounces them finds mercy.

Proverbs 28:13 (*NIV*)

(See also Romans 6:11–12 and Acts 3:19.)

* **List the sins that you wish you could stop committing.**

_____

_____

_____

_____

_____

_____

_____

* **What are the current consequences of your struggle with sin?**

_____

_____

_____

_____

_____

_____

closing prayer

Dear God, guide me to identify and choose those struggles that you want me to confess to you right here and now. Please give me the faith to believe in your mercy, grace, and love. Please give me the courage to approach you in my weakness and powerlessness. And please allow me to feel your love for me even when I feel no love for myself. Amen!

chapter 4

A MAN AFTER GOD'S OWN HEART

> *But now your kingdom will not endure; the Lord has sought out a man after his own heart and appointed him ruler of his people, because you have not kept the Lord's command.*
>
> **1 Samuel 13:14 (*NIV*)**

Throughout the Book of Psalms, King David provides one of the best examples in the Bible of how to bring struggles to God. David's prayers were always honest and real. He revealed all that was on his mind and in his heart to God. David shared his feelings and thoughts of love, frustration, anger, sadness, guilt, shame, pride, sin, failure, weakness, revenge, doubt, fear, and worry with God. He didn't hold anything back. He presented an example of a willing nakedness without shame before God. He let it all hang out, which is exactly what our God wants us to do before him. This is the meaning and ultimate purpose of confession.

> *There was a time when I wouldn't admit what a sinner I was. But my dishonesty made me miserable and filled my days with frustration. All day and all night your hand was heavy on me. My strength evaporated like water on a sunny day until I finally admitted all my sins to you and stopped trying to hide them. I said to myself, "I will confess them to the Lord." And you forgave me! All my guilt is gone.*
>
> **Psalm 32:3–5 (*TLB*)**

* **What current or past experiences, issues, or problems interfere with your relationship with God?**

_____

_____

_____

_____

_____

_____

King David was a murderer, an adulterer, a liar, a dysfunctional parent, an unfaithful husband, a polygamist, a slave-owner, and a hothead, yet and still God used him to further his kingdom. King David confessed it all to God, and God faithfully restored and empowered David to repent and do the right thing.

Create in me a pure heart, O God, and renew a steadfast spirit within me. Do not cast me from your presence or take your Holy Spirit from me. Restore to me the joy of your salvation and grant me a willing spirit, to sustain me.

Psalm 51:10–12 (NIV)

Have mercy on me, O God, according to your unfailing love; according to your great compassion blot out my transgressions. Wash away all my iniquity and cleanse me from my sin.

Psalm 51:1–2 (NIV)

* What difficulties do you have in opening your heart to God? What do you believe is causing this?

_____

_____

_____

_____

_____

_____

_____

_____

David is called a man after God's heart because he understood and accepted his complete dependence and absolute reliance upon God without reservation. God used David because he confessed and surrendered all to God, which is what allowed God to use him so powerfully. Consequently, there is much we can all learn from David's confessions.

* **What do you need to tell God that you've never told him before about what you truly and honestly feel, think, question, doubt, or believe?**

_____

_____

_____

_____

_____

_____

> *"Search me, O God, and know my heart; test me and know my anxious thoughts. Point out anything in me that offends you, and lead me along the path of everlasting life."*
>
> **Psalm 139:23–24 (*NLT*)**

* **What obstacles keep you from asking God to search you and know your heart?**

_____

_____

_____

_____

_____

_____

* **What secret or hidden things have you not confessed to God?**

_____

_____

_____

_____

_____

_____

* **What secret or hidden things have been done to you that you have not talked to God about? Why?**

_____

_____

_____

_____

_____

Your confession may cause you to worry, but you should never forget who your God is. Your God is love. Therefore, you have nothing to fear during this or any other Surrender Prayer step.

> *We know how much God loves us, and we have put our trust in his love. God is love, and all who live in love live in God, and God lives in them. And as we live in God, our love grows more perfect.... Such love has no fear, because perfect love expels all fear. If we are afraid, it is for fear of punishment, and this shows that we have not fully experienced his perfect love.*
>
> **1 John 4:16–18 (*NLT*)**

When we withhold our struggles from God, we prevent ourselves from experiencing his unsurpassed love for us. We fear confession because we believe that exposing our struggles to God will result in more pain and suffering. In other words, we mistakenly believe that our confessions will lead to God punishing us. But nowhere in the Bible does God state that we will be punished for confessing our struggles to him. On the contrary, the Bible provides countless examples of confession leading to forgiveness, love, mercy, and grace! Therefore, we can begin making real, honest, gut-level confessions to God so that we can begin to fully experience his unconditional love for us.

> *"Be strong and courageous. Do not be afraid; do not be discouraged, for the LORD your God will be with you wherever you go."*
>
> **Joshua 1:9 (*NIV*)**

* **Do you have a hard time believing that God is with you wherever you go? Why?**

_____

_____

_____

_____

_____

We not only confess those struggles that we played a role in creating, we also bring to God those struggles that exist in our lives through no fault of our own. When we experience issues related to injustice, abuse, neglect, poverty, trauma, loss, and the like, it is extremely difficult—if not impossible at times—to believe that God is with us. Nevertheless, we may also bring those issues to God in order to draw near to him.

* **What makes you feel separated from God?**

_____

_____

_____

_____

_____

_____

Our struggles do not separate us from God—it is our lack of willingness to offer our struggles to God that separates us from God. When we refuse to take our struggles to him, we—not God—are actively separating ourselves from him, and preventing him from drawing nearer to us. Consequently, we need to do our part and run to God when we struggle with our sin, weakness or powerlessness. When we do not go to him, we succeed in only making matters worse for ourselves.

* **Which of your struggles, obsessions, compulsions, addictions, sins, or wounds causes you the most pain and needs to be dealt with first?**

_____

_____

_____

_____

_____

_____

closing prayer

Dear God, please transform my heart so that I can be honest and real with you about all that I struggle with. I want you to be the first one I run to with my suffering and powerlessness. Help me overcome my fear of you because I no longer want to separate myself from your everlasting mercy, love and grace. Amen!

chapter 5

THE "WEAK"
AND
THE "STRONG"

> *He does not deal with us according to our sins,*
> *nor repay us according to our iniquities.*
> *For as high as the heavens are above the earth,*
> *so great is his steadfast love toward those who fear him;*
> *as far as the east is from the west,*
> *so far does he remove our transgressions from us.*
> *As a father shows compassion to his children,*
> *so the LORD shows compassion to those who fear him.*
>
> **Psalm 103:10–17 (*ESV*)**

The second step is Acceptance. As we grow in our knowledge of ourselves during the Prayer, we purposely and directly face our struggles with sin, weakness, and failure. We begin addressing the part of ourselves that makes us feel the most fear, anger, sadness, shame, or guilt. Acceptance is the realization that our struggle does not make us unforgivable, unlovable, or ugly. Acceptance is the realization that we are merely human and that we need God—nothing more and nothing less.

* **What makes you feel most ashamed, embarrassed, unworthy, or guilty?**

_____

_____

_____

_____

_____

_____

_____

The acceptance of our struggles is *never* an approval, rationalization, or excuse for our struggles. Our goal will always be the elimination of those aspects of ourselves that separate us from the love of God. Thus, we in no way desire to maintain or empower any aspect of ourselves that is contrary to God's will.

* **How have your struggles made you feel ashamed, embarrassed, unworthy, or guilty?**

_____

_____

_____

_____

_____

_____

_____

Self-acceptance is an understanding that what we struggle against is, and may always be, a part of us as a consequence of our human condition:

> *No matter which way I turn I can't make myself do right. I want to but I can't. When I want to do good, I don't; and when I try not to do wrong, I do it anyway....*
>
> *It seems to be a fact of life that when I want to do what is right, I inevitably do what is wrong. I love to do God's will so far as my new nature is concerned; but there is something else deep within me, in my lower nature, that is at war with my mind and wins the fight and makes me a slave to the sin that is still within me. In my mind I want to be God's willing servant, but instead I find myself still enslaved to sin.*
>
> **Romans 7:18–25 (TLB)**

Paul spoke clearly about his struggle with sin. Acceptance requires us to come to terms with such conflict. While on this earth, we can never eradicate our sinful nature—but we can learn how to claim progressive victory over it by engaging that part of us that genuinely wants to stop sinning, and by relying upon the power of God to set us free.

So you see how it is: my new life tells me to do right, but the old nature that is still inside me loves to sin. Oh, what a terrible predicament I'm in! Who will free me from my slavery to this deadly lower nature? Thank God! It has been done by Jesus Christ our Lord. He has set me free.

Romans 7:18–25 (TLB)

* Are there things about yourself that you hate or despise? Please list what they are.

_____

_____

_____

_____

_____

_____

* How have you harmed, punished, or put yourself down as a result of your self-hate?

_____

_____

_____

_____

_____

_____

_____

Our struggle with sin is, and always has been, the hallmark and expected consequence of a normal and authentic Christian walk. However, in most cases, the open and honest display of our struggles is no longer viewed as a virtue, but as a sign of weak faith or frail moral fiber. "Strong" Christians are celebrated, while "weak" Christians are rebuked, shunned, and rejected. This results in an inordinate amount of hidden sin and resultant pain. Today's message in most churches has denied reality. The truth is that there are no "strong" Christians; there are only "weak" ones who are choosing to bring their weakness into the light for divine healing to take place. Our weakness (or dependence upon God) should be celebrated—not rejected, hidden, or criticized. Once again, our example is the Apostle Paul who understood the relationship between our human weakness and God's strength:

> *I am going to boast only about how weak I am and how great God is to use such weakness for his glory.... Now I am glad to boast about how weak I am; I am glad to be a living demonstration of Christ's power, instead of showing off my own power and abilities. Since I know it is all for Christ's good, I am quite happy about "the thorn," and about insults and hardships, persecutions and difficulties; for when I am weak, then I am strong—the less I have, the more I depend on him.*
>
> **2 Corinthians 12:5–10 (*TLB*)**

* **What does the phrase "for when I am weak, then I am strong" mean to you?**

_____

_____

_____

_____

_____

_____

closing prayer

Dear God, please help me work through the shame, embarrassment, self-hate, and guilt that surround me when I think of my struggles. Please help me come to grips with my weakness. Help me to understand that my struggles do not make me less of a Christian or less deserving of your love and forgiveness. I don't want to hurt or punish myself anymore! I don't want to feel unworthy anymore. Allow me to see that I am only weak when I pretend to be strong. Teach me what true strength is in you. Amen!

chapter 6

HIDDEN STRUGGLES

When weakness is not brought into the light and accepted in the church, it remains hidden. It festers and spreads throughout the entire church body because church members do not receive the help they need for healing. The addict, the adulterer, the gossip, the abuser, the hypocrite, the depressed, the angry, the traumatized, the abused, the self-righteous, the racist, the misogynist, the mentally ill, and the lonely do not obtain the spiritual resources they need to overcome their struggles and receive the love of God. The shame surrounding their "weakness," prevents Christians from asking for help, which maintains and strengthens the spiritual strongholds that keep such Christians bound.

Within the context of this chapter, struggling Christians are individuals whose struggles make them feel looked down upon, pitied, ostracized, judged, embarrassed, or shamed by other Christians. They've unfortunately believed the falsehood communicated by some Christians that "good," "blessed," "righteous," or "strong" Christians do not struggle with the type of issues that struggling Christians battle. In addition, "struggling" Christians have often been led to believe by other Christians that they are *only* struggling because God is punishing them for some sin they've committed.

The disparagement of the struggling Christian in the church has led to incalculable harm, division, hypocrisy, and darkness in the Christian family of believers—starting with church leadership and ending with the congregation as a whole.

* **What are your deepest secrets?**

_____

_____

_____

_____

_____

_____

_____

_____

* **In your family of origin, was there a "family secret" that everyone tried to keep hidden? Please explain.**

_____

_____

_____

_____

_____

_____

Each Christian person constitutes a vital part of the whole church body. When any part of the body is bound, hurting, or in pain, the entire Christian family suffers and is weakened spiritually as a result:

> *[God] has made many parts for our bodies and has put each part just where he wants it.... And some of the parts that seem weakest and least important are really the most necessary.... So God has put the body together in such a way that extra honor and care are given to those parts that might otherwise seem less important. This makes for happiness among the parts, so that the parts have the same care for each other that they do for themselves. If one part suffers, all parts suffer with it, and if one part is honored, all the parts are glad. Now here is what I am trying to say: All of you together are the one body of Christ, and each one of you is a separate and necessary part of it.*
>
> **1 Corinthians 12:18–27 (*TLB*)**

It is the church's responsibility to do everything it can to acknowledge, accept, help, and love all of its members—especially those members who possess weaknesses that the majority of churches would rather ignore, judge, or condemn. The church is only as strong as its presumed weakest link. Accordingly, the church will never be spiritually healthy as long as it continues to reject its supposed "weak" or "less important" parts.

* **What memories have you tried to deny or hide from yourself, from others, and from God? Why?**

_____

_____

_____

_____

_____

_____

_____

* **What behaviors have you tried to deny or hide from yourself, from others, and from God? Why?**

_____

_____

_____

_____

_____

_____

* **What feelings have you tried to deny or hide from yourself, from others, and from God? Why?**

_____

_____

_____

_____

_____

_____

* **What thoughts have you tried to deny or hide from yourself, from others, and from God? Why?**

_____

_____

_____

_____

_____

_____

* **What sins have you tried to deny or hide from yourself, from others, and from God? Why?**

_____

_____

_____

_____

_____

_____

* **What trauma, abuse or neglect have you tried to deny or hide from yourself, from others, and from God? Why?**

_____

_____

_____

_____

_____

_____

_____

* **What other issues, problems, conflicts, weaknesses or struggles have you tried to deny or hide from yourself, from others, and from God? Why?**

_____

_____

_____

_____

_____

* **How has what you've tried to keep hidden and secret negatively affected your life? When you've hidden your struggles, what negative consequences have resulted?**

_____

_____

_____

_____

_____

* Has your denial ever isolated you from your most important relationships?

_____

_____

_____

_____

_____

_____

Acceptance requires you to embrace your weakness as Paul did. You are not defective, and nothing is wrong with you. You are God's child—and God fully accepts you for all that you are. When we become able to accept ourselves, we learn to embrace all that we are in the same manner that our Lord and Savior Jesus Christ does. We ultimately learn to love ourselves because God first loved us. (Romans 5:8, 8:31–39)

* What struggles have caused you to compromise your values, convictions, and self-esteem? How have they done so?

_____

_____

_____

_____

_____

_____

* How have your struggles demonized, shamed, or embarrassed yourself or others?

_____

_____

_____

_____

_____

* What are you unwilling or unable to accept about yourself? Why?

_____

_____

_____

_____

_____

* What have been the consequences of this lack of acceptance?

_____

_____

_____

_____

_____

_____

* **What are you unwilling or unable to forgive yourself for? Why?**

_____

_____

_____

_____

_____

_____

* **What have been the consequences for this lack of forgiveness?**

_____

_____

_____

_____

_____

_____

Jesus died for us while we were still sinners. He performed the ultimate act of love on our behalf to show us that he loved us in spite of our weaknesses and failings. He didn't die for us because of anything we achieved or did right—

he died for us to prove that his love was not conditioned upon any imagined "righteousness" on our parts. If we could attain righteousness on our own, Jesus never would have been crucified. The Acceptance step requires us to cast off the pretense of being "good" or "strong" Christians, and shows us how to get real with ourselves, with God, and with each other.

* **Does your walk as a Christian match your talk? Are your actions the same at recovery meetings, church, home, and work? Why or why not?**

_____

_____

_____

_____

_____

* **In what ways are you dishonest with yourself, with others, and with God concerning your struggles?**

_____

_____

_____

_____

_____

_____

* **How does your pride or fear keep you from being honest with yourself about your struggles? What are you afraid of facing?**

_____

_____

_____

_____

_____

_____

* **In what areas of your life do you suspect that denial about your struggles is most active? How do you lie to yourself about your struggles? Why?**

_____

_____

_____

_____

_____

_____

When we begin to grasp the significance of God's acceptance, we will begin to understand the depths of his love for us. We will realize that his unconditional acceptance of all that we are is an expression of his unconditional love.

In other words, God loves you when you are "good"; God loves you when you are "bad." He loves you no matter what's been done to you; no matter what you've done; no matter what you're doing; and no matter what you are going to do in the future. He won't love you any more for being a "good" Christian, or any less for being a "bad" Christian. God does not want you to prove that you are worthy of such love. God does not want you to think that you have to earn such love. God just wants you to love him back, which will require you to learn how to surrender. (This final step of the Surrender Prayer will be discussed in the "Surrender Step" chapters.)

closing prayer

Dear God, help me get real with you. I'm tired of faking it in our relationship and in my relationships with others. Teach me and empower me to begin the process of overcoming my secrets, my denial, and my pride. I don't want to hide from you anymore! So please give me the strength to defeat my fear. Amen!

chapter 7

SITTING WITH OUR JUNK

Understanding God's acceptance is an essential element of the Surrender Prayer. If we know that God accepts us unconditionally, we know that we can begin to accept ourselves unconditionally. We can unmask ourselves in his presence—and stand naked before him as Adam and Eve did in the garden. This means that we can learn to bring anything before him. And <u>anything</u> truly means <u>anything</u>—after all, he knows everything we feel, think, and do anyway.

* **What fears surface when you realize God knows all your faults?**

_____

_____

_____

_____

_____

The Acceptance step completely contradicts the belief that a person should be able to get over it, or be able to "let it go" without first owning his or her issues. Before you can let something go, you have to first discover it, grasp it, examine it, process it, and finally embrace it—because "it" is a part of you. You need to integrate the part of yourself that causes you so much distress before you can ever be freed from the power that it holds over you. There are no shortcuts. This embrace takes courage, strength, resilience, and faith in a God that accepts and loves you unconditionally for all that you are.

The embrace of our struggle is an acceptance of our struggle with the understanding that our Lord and Savior is beside us throughout the entire process—accepting and loving us through the pain, sadness, and anxiety that we experience as a result of our struggle. When we face, accept, and sit with our struggles, we are facing, accepting and sitting with our "junk": those issues, problems, temptations, addictions, cravings, and destructive thoughts and emotions that we believe compel us to act out in some manner that is harmful to ourselves and to those around us.

"Sitting with our junk" is by no means a pleasurable experience. It requires us to come face-to-face with the pain that we have attempted to avoid for so long.

* **What are you trying to escape and not face?**

_____

_____

_____

_____

_____

* **In what ways have you attempted to escape from the pain of your struggles and weaknesses?**

_____

_____

_____

_____

_____

_____

* How are you distracting yourself from the pain of your struggles and weaknesses?

_____

_____

_____

_____

_____

* How have your self-medicating behaviors, old survival techniques, and defense mechanisms failed you in dealing with your pain and struggles?

_____

_____

_____

_____

_____

* **Do your struggles with addiction, unhealthy behaviors, or sin cover up other deeper (secret or hidden) struggles, problems, or issues that you have not yet confronted?**

_____

_____

_____

_____

_____

* **What struggles, problems, or issues were you originally attempting to escape with unhealthy bad habits or harmful compulsive behaviors?**

_____

_____

_____

_____

_____

When we accept and sit with our junk, we begin to weaken the powerful hold that it has over our lives. We discover that our destructive obsessions, compulsions, cravings, and temptations are not all-powerful. We learn that merely thinking about (or feeling like) doing something harmful does not mean that we have to do that something. The Prayer enables us to see through the big lie that we are powerless to resist the harmful acting out behaviors of our addictions, weaknesses, cravings, temptations, sins, and failures. We discover that we can sit with our struggles without acting out immediately in inevitably harmful ways.

* **In what ways do you feel powerless or weak in dealing with your emotions such as resentment, sadness or anger?**

_____

_____

_____

_____

_____

* **What emotions do you have difficulty expressing?**

_____

_____

_____

_____

_____

For example:
- A drug addict will learn that he can sit with the craving to pop a pill and not have to "use."
- A man who struggles with social anxiety will learn that he can sit with his fear of social situations and not be forced to isolate or alienate himself from others.
- A porn addict will learn that she can sit with her desire to lust and not have to act out to on-line pornography.
- A food addict will learn to sit with his compulsion to binge and not have to eat until he feels like his belly will burst.
- A woman who struggles with explosive anger will learn to sit

with that anger and not lash out unjustly at those whom she loves
the most.

- A people-pleaser will learn to sit with his desire to say "yes" to everyone and not have to continue being exploited by others.
- And a woman who suffers from PTSD will learn to "sit" with her flashbacks and not have them inevitably result in a panic attack.

As we learn to "sit" with our struggles, we learn to be still and know God (Psalm 46:10). By developing a space and time for God's presence and power to penetrate, this "sitting" creates a buffer of time between what you are tempted to do—but struggling not to do—and your resultant, reflexive, seemingly automatic response to actually do the very thing that you are struggling not to do. We discover a calm within the storm of our waging internal desires:

> *Do not be anxious about anything, but in every situation, by prayer and petition, with thanksgiving, present your requests to God. And the peace of God, which transcends all understanding, will guard your hearts and your minds in Christ Jesus.*
>
> **Philippians 4:6–7 (NIV)**

closing prayer

Dear God, teach me how to sit with my "junk." Let me begin to embrace all that I am, knowing that you embrace me for all that I am. Prove to me that I can think what I think and feel what I feel without having to hurt others or myself. Give me the faith to believe that you are by my side protecting me when I am overwhelmed with temptation, sadness, anxiety, or any struggle. Show me how to face myself. Amen!

chapter 8

PAIN MANAGEMENT

The Acceptance Step teaches us to tolerate our pain, weakness, sin, and failings because we learn how to face that which we fear. We learn to manage the hurtful feelings, thoughts, and memories that we deny. And we discover that we no longer have to resort to destructive behaviors (drugs, sex, alcohol, anger, gambling, abuse, neglect, isolation, pornography, masturbation, cutting, excessive exercise, anorexia, binging, purging, and the like) to self-medicate.

* **What behaviors do you use to compensate for or cover your uncomfortable feelings, thoughts, or memories?**

_____

_____

_____

_____

_____

_____

* **List the things you have used to block the pain of your past.**

_____

_____

_____

_____

_____

* **In what ways do you medicate, distract yourself from, or seek to escape your pain with alcohol, drugs, sex, eating, shopping, gambling, or some other unhealthy, compulsive behavior?**

_____

_____

_____

_____

* **How do these behaviors affect your relationships with others?**

_____

_____

_____

_____

* **How do these behaviors affect any other aspect of your life?**

_____

_____

_____

_____

_____

Our self-medicating behaviors are survival skills that were created, fostered, and reinforced in response to our unhealthy environments and traumatic life experiences. Most of us had no alternative but to develop such coping strategies because we were never exposed to or taught healthy coping strategies. We had no one to show us how to depend upon the power of God to get us through another year, month, week, day, hour, minute, or second without resorting to a destructive escape. Please realize that God understands this—and does not judge or condemn you for your attempts at coping.

> *Therefore, since we have a great high priest who has ascended into heaven, Jesus the Son of God, let us hold firmly to the faith we profess. For we do not have a high priest who is unable to empathize with our weaknesses, but we have one who has been tempted in every way, just as we are—yet he did not sin. Let us then approach God's throne of grace with confidence, so that we may receive mercy and find grace to help us in our time of need.*
> **Hebrews 4:14–16 (*NIV*)**

* **In what ways have you avoided addressing your unhealthy behaviors, sins, or struggles? Why?**

_____

_____

_____

_____

_____

* **Do you excuse, justify, defend, or rationalize your unhealthy behaviors, sins, or struggles? How? Why?**

_____

_____

_____

_____

_____

This process of freeing ourselves from the "yoke" of our unhealthy self-medicating behaviors will take time and effort, but Christ has already assured us the victory in this battle.

> *For freedom Christ has set us free; stand firm there-*
> *fore, and do not submit again to a yoke of slavery.*
> **Galatians 5:1 (*ESV*)**

When you confront your struggle, you will encounter the good, the bad, and the ugly that lie within you. You will uncover your subconscious thoughts and feelings. Old memories and experiences—both pleasurable and traumatic—will be brought out into the open and into God's light. This journey of acceptance will at times cause you discomfort or sadness. But you will learn to accept, without judgment, all that you experience during the Surrender Prayer so that your feelings and thoughts will no longer have the power to entangle, overwhelm, define, or control you. In a sense, you will become a mindful observer of your inner struggle by learning to: (1) acknowledge your struggle; (2) accept your inner struggle without judging yourself; and (3) sit with your inner struggle without becoming entangled in, or overwhelmed by, it.

For example, when a pornography addict takes his struggle with pornography to God during the Awareness step, his mind may, at times, become flooded with uninvited, graphic, sexual images. The man may even experience an unwelcome level of arousal as a result of the images. These images will be frightening because the part of the man that is conditioned to begin acting out in a harmful and unhealthy way will be tempted to do so. But this will be in direct conflict with the other part of the man that began practicing the Surrender Prayer for the express purpose of learning how to overcome his pornography addiction.

Put more simply, an all too familiar internal battle will take place between the man's desire to do wrong and his desire to do right. The part of him that desires to do wrong will want to indulge and be swept away by the images and act out in harmful lust. The part of him that wants to do right will want to escape, deny, and disassociate from the images by any means necessary.

The part that wants to do right can be retrained to do the opposite of what he has taught himself to do to resist temptation in the past. He can learn a new way to fight his temptations because his old way of fighting has ultimately failed him. The Acceptance step provides this new way of resisting the temptation to act out with the images.

While moving through the Acceptance Step, when encountering such images, this man will no longer: (1) freak out or become overwhelmed by the fear that he will fall into temptation yet again, (2) become engrossed in the images, (3) masturbate, (4) discontinue the Surrender Prayer, or (5) in anyway actively attempt to escape or distract himself from the images. Instead, he will simply sit with the images.

When he sits in the presence of the graphic images, he learns to be still with the images by acknowledging and accepting their existence. When he acknowledges the images, he takes ownership of his struggle, and actively decides not to run away from it. He makes the decision to spiritually confront his struggle—and may later even learn to embrace it.

> *Consider it pure joy, my brothers and sisters, whenever you face trials of many kinds, because you know that the testing of your faith produces perseverance. Let perseverance finish its work so that you may be mature and complete, not lacking anything.*
>
> **James 1:2–4 (NIV)**

He takes a stand and announces that he doesn't have to let the fear of being led into sin control his reaction to such images. Through this process, he begins to see that the images are only images; and that such images by themselves have no magical power to compel him to act out in a sexually harmful or unhealthy way.

By accepting the images, he is not approving of (or feeling any delight in) their presence. Nor is he actively poring over the images in lust. He is accepting the fact that this is his struggle; and while his struggle does not define who he is, his struggle will be a part of who he is until such time that God removes it from him. He is learning to be mindful about, and even make peace with, that part of him that is the struggle. He continues to actively fight the struggle, but he is learning a new way to do battle.

Again, the acceptance of his struggle is never an approval of his struggle, but the recognition that he can encounter, confront, and overcome his struggle with God by his side. Therefore, when the man sits in acceptance with his struggle, he is symbolically telling it to "Take your best shot!" because he now has faith in God's power to withstand whatever temptation the images bring his way.

If the man is sincere in his desire to resist his struggle with pornography, his Acceptance step will segue into the third and final step of the Surrender Prayer (the Surrender Step), which will pull God into the man's struggle so that God can begin fighting the images for him. In a very real sense, the Acceptance step fulfills the precondition of learning how to be still so that God can begin fighting for him.

> *"The Lord will fight for you; you need only to be still."*
> **Exodus 14:14 (NIV)**

Please remember that when we confront our struggles during the Acceptance step, we strive to do so without self-judgment. No matter what images, thoughts, feelings, or memories pop up in our brains, we begin to fully accept ourselves during the Prayer. Why? First, even though we gain the tools to manage the unwelcome and uninvited images, thoughts, feelings, and memories that pop into our heads during the Prayer, we quickly realize that we have no power or control over when, where, why, or how these images, thoughts, feelings and memories initially materialize.

Second, it is pointless for any of us to condemn or judge ourselves for our inability to ever completely disconnect from our struggles with temptation, sin, depression, disordered eating, low self-esteem, or any other problem because our struggles are an unavoidable, expected and natural component of life. Whether we like it or not, struggles will be a permanent part of our existence. Our struggles with temptation, oppression, trauma, anger, and sadness will never be entirely eliminated, but will be overcome through our faith and daily reliance upon the power of our God. (Please review Romans 7:14–25.)

Third, you've judged and condemned yourself enough over the years— and it has never enabled you to overcome your struggles. For the fifteen minutes that you practice the Surrender Prayer, give yourself permission to be:

- kind to yourself,
- loving to yourself, and
- accepting of yourself.

When your prayer session is complete, you may return to the baggage of self-condemnation and self-judgment if you choose. Or, you may decide to begin believing that all your self-judgment and self-condemnation may *not* be what God wants for you.

closing prayer

Dear God, give me the strength to resist the temptation to run to my unhealthy self-medicating behaviors when I am in pain. Please give me the courage to face my struggles when I am in prayer with you. Show me how to be still in the battle so that you can fight for me. When I am tempted to return to my old, ineffective ways of fighting temptation, please give me the faith to believe that you are there, ready and waiting, to do battle on my behalf. Amen.

chapter 9

"WHITE–KNUCKLING," DISTRACTIONS, AND YOUR SPIRITUAL ANCHOR

When we choose to reject our struggles instead of accepting them, we make it impossible to overcome them. When we disassociate from, block out, or deny our struggles, we expend an ever-increasing amount of energy to maintain the delusion that we can somehow ignore or separate ourselves from our pain or problems. We continually drain our limited human resources to fight a battle that we will eventually lose, every time. Consequently, the more energy and effort we expend to reject any part of ourselves, the more powerful such part becomes.

This fighting method is known as "white–knuckling," or combating our struggles by sheer willpower. When we white–knuckle our recovery, we are depending solely upon our own strength—not God's—to overcome our struggles. Consequently, when we white–knuckle our recovery, we do not experience the fruit of the Holy Spirit (love, joy, peace, forbearance, kindness, goodness, faithfulness, gentleness, and self control) in ever-increasing abundance. We, instead, experience an increasing level of stress, anxiety, anger, resentment, confusion, greed, lust, jealousy, envy, selfishness, irritability, fatigue, or hopelessness.

"Pressure busts pipes" is a common refrain in recovery parlance. Through acceptance, we learn to release the pressure of our struggles—not increase it. This acceptance is a form of spiritual aikido: we use the power of our struggle against itself. When we are confronted by our struggle, we no longer empower it by directly resisting it through various forms of rejection, denial, or escapism. We sit with our struggle, acknowledge it and accept it, which, in turn, disempowers it.

During the process of sitting with your struggle, you will inevitably experience distractions. As you sit still in acceptance with your struggles, you will quickly discover that your mind will do anything to distract you from stillness. What are the distractions? Anything that your mind can conjure to fight being still: bills, sex, drugs, lust, alcohol, fear, doubt, frustration, resentment, disgust, anger, embarrassment, ideas, images, friendships, trauma, doubts, to-do-lists, children, relationships, jobs, appointments, future plans, impatience, vacations, exercise, movies—anything!

We may be surprised at what comes up, but we do not fall into the distraction trap by giving up on the Acceptance step. When the distractions come, please remember that whatever arises is okay. We do not reject or deny our distractions. Nor do we condemn or judge ourselves for their existence. Rather, we acknowledge and accept our distractions in the same manner that we acknowledge and accept our struggles. Ironically, the more we actively attempt not to accept our distractions, the greater chance that we become overwhelmed and entangled by them.

If and when we become overwhelmed by thoughts, emotions, or distractions during the Surrender Prayer, we utilize our spiritual anchor. Our anchor represents our spiritual connection to God. It represents our belief that we remain in his presence. It is our reminder that we are not alone—that the Lord "is our refuge and strength, an ever-present help in times of trouble" (Psalm 46:1). We use our anchor in the Acceptance step to ground ourselves in Jesus. Whenever we feel distracted or overwhelmed by our feelings, thoughts, or memories, we turn to our anchor to help center ourselves within the love and protection of our Savior. Whenever we experience self-disgust, self-doubt, hopelessness, fear, anxiety, sadness, anger, or resentment, we use our anchor as a means to focus our hearts, minds, spirits, and souls upon the presence and power of God. When you confront your inner struggle, your anchor represents your faith and hope that your God is always there to protect you, love you and keep you safe—no matter what.

Your anchor may be as short as one word, or as long as a few words. Examples include: "Jesus," "Help," "Love," "God," "Save me," "Help me," "Love me," or verses such as "The Lord is my strength and shield." We select our anchor before we begin the Prayer practice; and, once selected, we do not change it during our prayer session. You may need to test different anchors before you find one that best suits you, but please do not get stuck trying to find the perfect anchor—there is no such thing. Try out your selected anchor for at least one entire session before deciding, if necessary, to change it. The significance and meaning that we ascribe to our anchor are what make the anchor special—the actual words we choose to represent the anchor are far less important.

* **What have you selected as your spiritual anchor? Please provide at least three possibilities.**

_____

_____

_____

_____

_____

_____

closing prayer

Father, I pray that you give me the strength to face my struggles, and that you also provide me with the courage to begin accepting all that I am—just as you accept all that I am. Please show me what it means to be unconditionally loved and accepted by you. Please give me the faith to believe that you will never reject me or stop loving me. I no longer want to run away from the painful thoughts, feelings, temptations, and memories that keep me imprisoned. Help me to perceive your loving presence by my side as I stop running from the parts of myself that hurt me. Please protect me as I face my weaknesses, dysfunction, and pain. And please help me understand and believe that the struggles I now confront in faith have never made me ugly, unlovable, unforgivable, irredeemable, or unworthy in your sight. Amen!

chapter 10

"I GIVE UP!"

> *"Do not be afraid. Stand firm and you will see the deliverance the Lord will bring you today. The Egyptians you see today you will never see again. The Lord will fight for you; you need only to be still."*
>
> **Exodus 14:13 (*NIV*)**

Through awareness, we learn to identify our struggles. Through acceptance, we learn to sit with our struggles. Through surrender, we learn to overcome our struggles by accessing the power of the Holy Spirit.

Surrender requires us to realize that all prior attempts to overcome the entrenched problem areas of our lives have ended in failure. Our life experiences have taught us that we can't overcome our physical, emotional, cognitive, and spiritual enemies with our own strength, abilities, or willpower. When we surrender, we don't surrender to our physical, emotional, mental and spiritual foes—we surrender (or hand over) our fight to God, and get him to do the fighting for us. True surrender requires us to learn how to completely depend upon the power of the Holy Spirit to fight our battles:

> *Don't you yet understand? Don't you know by now that the everlasting God, the Creator of the farthest parts of the earth, never grows faint or weary? No one can fathom the depths of his understanding. He gives power to the tired and worn out, and strength to the weak. Even the youths shall be exhausted, and the young men will all give up. But they that wait upon the Lord shall renew their strength. They shall mount up with wings like eagles; they shall run and not be weary; they shall walk and not faint.*
>
> **Isaiah 40:28–31 (TLB)**

> *Humble yourselves, therefore, under God's mighty hand, that he may lift you up in due time. Cast all your anxiety on him because he cares for you.*
>
> **1 Peter 5:6–7 (NIV)**

* **What struggles in your life make you feel powerless?**

_____

_____

_____

_____

_____

* What circumstances have you tried to change but have realized that you cannot change no matter how much you wish you could?

_____

_____

_____

_____

_____

* List those struggles, wounds, and problems that you wish you could "get over" or recover from?

_____

_____

_____

_____

_____

* What in your past has caused you to have the "If onlys"? For example: "If only" I had stopped _____ years ago; or "If only" _____ hadn't left me.

_____

_____

_____

_____

_____

_____

* **Describe the ways that you have tried and failed to fix yourself using your own strength?**

_____

_____

_____

_____

_____

The reality of our lives clearly illustrates that we have been overwhelmed and overpowered on many occasions. However, our reality also demonstrates that we have somehow miraculously survived life's trials relatively intact. Our survival is a testament to God's love, mercy, and grace—not to our own spiritual, physical, or emotional fortitude. In fact, for most of us, God has preserved our lives—and our sanity—in spite of our many bad decisions.

* **Have you been trusting God to remove your struggles or are you relying on your own willpower to change? Why?**

_____

_____

_____

_____

_____

_____

_____

* What doubts do you have about God helping you overcome your struggles?

_____

_____

_____

_____

_____

* In the past, pain has triggered us to act out our addictions, obsessions, and compulsions. Pain can now be our signal to recognize our powerlessness and choose to become empowered by the Holy Spirit. What specific pains are your biggest triggers?

_____

_____

_____

_____

_____

* **What struggles have you come to realize require God to come in and fix? What do you need God to battle for you?**

_____

_____

_____

_____

_____

_____

_____

Our surrender to God is an acknowledgement that he has sustained us through every storm—whether we have realized this fact or not. When we surrender to God, we admit that we are powerless over our struggles, and we consent to allow God to move through us so that he can begin fighting for us. God requires this consent because he has given us all free will. He will not force us to choose him, to love him, or to obey him. He did not create robots. The spirit that he has placed in each one of us represents God's desire to establish a true relationship with us: a relationship based upon friendship. Yes, God wants to be your friend:

> _"I no longer call you servants, because a servant does not know his master's business. Instead, I have called you friends, for everything that I learned from my Father I have made known to you."_
>
> **John 15:15 (_NIV_)**

* **What area of your life do you believe will be the most difficult to surrender? In what area of your life do you experience the strongest need to be in control?**

_____

_____

_____

_____

_____

_____

* **What in your past is keeping you from seeking and following God's will for your life?**

_____

_____

_____

_____

_____

This relationship requires us to make a choice. Everyday (indeed, every waking moment) we have on this earth requires us all to make a conscious choice of whom we shall follow:

> *If it is disagreeable in your sight to serve the LORD, choose for yourselves today whom you will serve: whether the gods which your fathers served which were beyond the River, or the gods of the Amorites in whose land you are living; but as for me and my house, we will serve the LORD.*
>
> **Joshua 24:15 (*NASB*)**

Our daily decision to follow God and stay surrendered to him requires us to let go of our attempts at controlling ourselves, our lives, our will and our current circumstances. There is nothing easy about surrender. In fact, choosing to surrender day in and day out—even when we don't feel like doing it—runs contrary to everything that our world has taught us to do in order to survive. That is, our experiences have conditioned most of us not to put our complete trust in anyone or anything because we've been hurt so badly when we've done so in the past.

> *Surrender your heart to God, turn to him in prayer, and give up your sins—even those you do in secret. Then you won't be ashamed; you will be confident and fearless.*
>
> **Job 11:13–15 (*CEV*)**

There will always be a fearful, defiant, resistant, doubtful, or willful part of us that will not want to surrender. But God isn't looking for a 100%, one-time, perfect surrender. All he requires is a part of you—no matter how small—that is willing to step out in faith to trust him one day at a time. Whatever you choose to willingly surrender to God is a sufficient starting point for a brand new relationship with him. So please be encouraged to move past your fear. God is waiting for you!

closing prayer

Father, I give up! I realize that I can't overcome my struggles on my own. But I am afraid. Will you be there for me? You have to show me that I can trust you with my struggles. You have to show me that you care. I've been hurt so badly. I'm in so much pain. God, give me the courage to surrender to you. Give me the faith to believe that the willing part of me—no matter how small—is more than enough for you to welcome me into your arms. Amen!

chapter 11

GOD DOESN'T LOVE THE WAY WE LOVE

We worship a God who willingly chose to go to the cross to prove his love to us. Jesus didn't have to do it. He could have walked away from the cross and our redemption—but he didn't because he doesn't love the way that we love. He loves us in a way that we can never love each other. He loves us in a way that we can never love him. He loves us with a love that we will never fully comprehend:

> *Who shall separate us from the love of Christ? Shall tribulation, or distress, or persecution, or famine, or nakedness, or danger, or sword? As it is written, "For your sake we are being killed all the day long; we are regarded as sheep to be slaughtered." No, in all these things we are more than conquerors through him who loved us. For I am sure that neither death nor life, nor angels nor rulers, nor things present nor things to come, nor powers, nor height nor depth, nor anything else in all creation, will be able to separate us from the love of God in Christ Jesus our Lord.*
>
> **Romans 8:35–39 (ESV)**

When we surrender our struggle to God, we may surrender with confidence because we know who our God is. In fact, we may boldly approach God in our times of need:

> *So let us come boldly to the throne of our gracious God. There we will receive his mercy, and we will find grace to help us when we need it most.*
>
> **Hebrews 4:16 (*NLT*)**

* **What doubts do you have about God's love for you?**

_____

_____

_____

_____

_____

* **What was your childhood relationship like with God?**

_____

_____

_____

_____

_____

_____

* How do your childhood memories frighten or otherwise affect you negatively?

_____

_____

_____

_____

_____

_____

* Does your difficulty in trusting God or fearing God have anything to do with your childhood relationships with your parents or any childhood trauma?

_____

_____

_____

_____

_____

_____

* Which area of your childhood needs the most healing?

_____

_____

_____

_____

_____

_____

At times, we may fail to fully grasp that we worship a suffering God: that we actually worship a God who not only feels his own pain, temptations, anguish, and despair, but all of ours as well.

> *Then Jesus went with them to a place called Gethsemane, and he said to his disciples, "Sit here, while I go over there and pray." And taking with him Peter and the two sons of Zebedee, he began to be sorrowful and troubled. Then he said to them, "My soul is very sorrowful, even to death; remain here, and watch with me." And going a little farther he fell on his face and prayed, saying, "My Father, if it be possible, let this cup pass from me; nevertheless, not as I will, but as you will."*
>
> **Matthew 26:36–39 (*ESV*)**

> *For we do not have a high priest who is unable to empathize with our weaknesses, but we have one who has been tempted in every way, just as we are— yet he did not sin.*
>
> **Hebrews 4:15 (*NIV*)**

> *For this reason he had to be made like them, fully human in every way, in order that he might become a merciful and faithful high priest in service to God, and that he might make atonement for the sins of the people. Because he himself suffered when he was tempted, he is able to help those who are being tempted.*
>
> **Hebrews 2:17–18 (*NIV*)**

(See also John 11:32–36, Matthew 27:46, Luke 22:39–44, and Luke 4:1–2)

The significance of Jesus Christ feeling our pain is this: when we suffer, Jesus suffers with us. When we hurt, Jesus hurts. When we are in pain, Jesus is in pain. When we are beaten, raped, molested, abused, lied to, starved, dying, oppressed, insulted, enslaved, bruised, or tempted, Jesus is right there with us feeling and experiencing everything that we feel and experience.

> *Surely he took up our pain and bore our suffering, yet we considered him punished by God, stricken by him, and afflicted.*
>
> **Isaiah 53:4 (*NIV*)**

Our God does not dispassionately sit on a distant, golden throne in heaven callously removed from our struggles. Our God is not some sadistic, omnipotent being who idly watches us go through our struggles while waiting for the next opportunity to "zap" us with lightening when we do wrong. No, our God is right here. Right here in the pain—in your pain, in my pain, in the entire world's pain.

> *In all their distress he too was distressed, and the angel of his presence saved them.*
> *In his love and mercy he redeemed them; he lifted them up and carried them all the days of old.*
>
> **Isaiah 63:9 (*NIV*)**

> *You keep track of all my sorrows. You have collected all my tears in your bottle.*
> *You have recorded each one in your book.*
>
> **Psalm 56:8 (*NLT*)**

The ultimate expression and proof of God's love for us is his voluntary union with us in the pain and despair of our struggles. There is no greater love than this.

closing prayer

Dear God, reveal your love to me. Help me understand it, and teach me how to accept it. Give me the faith to believe that you've not only been with me during my painful struggles, but that you've also experienced all of the pain that I've experienced during my struggles. Amen!

chapter 12

GETTING REAL WITH GOD

Owning our struggles requires us to be completely open and honest with God and ourselves about every thought, desire, feeling, doubt, and question we may have. When we get honest with God, we finally start getting real with God. We put everything on the table, and we let God have it all. We don't hold anything back.

We let him know exactly how we feel. We share our heartache, our pain, our desperation, our anger, our resentment, and our weakness with him. If there is a part of us that doesn't want to resist our struggle, we tell him. If there is a part of us that wants to sin, hurt ourselves, or hurt others, we tell him. If we are mad at God, we tell him. If we are disgusted with our lives or with God, we tell him. If we don't understand why there is so much pain in our lives and in the world, we tell him. If we think that God is unfair or unjust, we tell him. If we doubt his existence or love, we tell him. If we believe that the world is unfair, we tell him. If we blame God for our pain, addiction, illness, obsession, compulsion, failure or struggle, we tell him. If there is a part of us that wants to get high, look at on-line porn, hit our wives or our children, commit adultery, commit a crime, lie, or give-up on God or ourselves; we tell him.

* **What scares me most about sharing all of my struggles, sins, doubts, and darkness with God?**

_____

_____

_____

_____

_____

We own and embrace all that we think and feel during the Prayer by communicating all that we think and feel to God. We confess it all, and let it out so that we can learn to let it go. God won't force us to give it to him, we first have to hand it over to him willingly. This letting go is an essential element of our surrender to God. We stop holding onto it, and allow God to take it from us.

Don't worry. Don't fear. God can handle your surrender. God won't punish you for expressing your thoughts and feelings—he already knows what your thoughts and feelings are anyway. And God will still love you after you surrender it all to him. In fact, you will experience more of his love after you realize that God accepts and loves you no matter what you feel or think about him or anyone else.

closing prayer

Dear God, give me the courage to get real with you. I don't want to be afraid of being totally honest with you anymore. I want to be completely unguarded and uncovered before you. Give me the strength to break through the shame, guilt, and embarrassment that I feel about those things I've done, felt, and thought so that I can give it all to you. And please, Father, give me the faith to believe that you will accept and love me for all that I am—and will not punish, condemn or judge me. Thank you, Jesus! Amen.

chapter 13

HOW IT WORKS

When we surrender our struggles to God, we depend upon God exclusively to empower us to overcome our struggles. We do not actually stop fighting—we just stop fighting in our own strength. We let go, stop resisting in our own power, and immerse ourselves in the grace of our Lord and Savior, Jesus. This means that we stop using our own limited resources to fight for ourselves, and begin tapping into the unlimited power reserves of our higher power. In other words, we gradually remove our strength from the conflict while intentionally drawing God's strength into the conflict. We become less to allow God to become so much more. As we let go of our fight, we trust God's Spirit to instruct, empower, strengthen, and direct us in the battle:

> *For it is God who works in you to will and to act according to his good purpose.*
>
> **Philippians 2:13 (*NIV*)**

> *Not that we are competent in ourselves to claim anything for ourselves, but our competence comes from God.*
>
> **2 Corinthians 3:5 (*NIV*)**

> *Fear not, for I am with you. Do not be dismayed. I am your God. I will strengthen you; I will help you; I will uphold you with my victorious right hand.*
>
> **Isaiah 41:10 (*TLB*)**

(See also Proverbs 3:5–6, Psalm 143:10–11, Matthew 7:7, Psalm 119:105–106, Isaiah 30:21, Psalm 25:8–11, Matthew 11:28–30, Psalm 118:8–9, 2 Thessalonians 3:3, Psalm 119:10–12, and Psalm 25:4–5.)

* **In your struggles, how do you fight surrendering them to God? How do you block God from fighting for you?**

_____

_____

_____

_____

_____

* **How has life been unfair to you? How has God let you down or disappointed you?**

_____

_____

_____

_____

_____

_____

* **List examples of when you doubted God. What were the consequences of your doubt?**

_____

_____

_____

_____

_____

* **Describe the times in your life when you took control away from God because of your doubts?**

_____

_____

_____

_____

_____

We will experience some level of fear when we first stop resisting our struggle because the urges, cravings, feelings, and thoughts that arise did, in fact, previously have the power to compel us to act out in harmful ways. There will be a part of us that will want to run away from and block out what we encounter, but please remember that God is always there with us:

> *Do not be anxious about anything, but in every situation, by prayer and petition, with thanksgiving, present your requests to God. And the peace of God, which transcends all understanding, will guard your hearts and your minds in Christ Jesus.*
>
> **Philippians 4:6–7 (*NIV*)**

The issues and problems that we surrender to God will determine what we encounter during our Prayer practice. For example:

- The sex addict will experience lustful feelings, images, and memories.
- The drug addict will be struck by drug cravings.
- The alcoholic will be hit with strong urges to drink alcohol.
- The gambling addict will be triggered to gamble.
- Those who suffer from feelings of low self-worth will encounter instances of neglect, abandonment, or abuse.
- Those who suffer from anxiety may revisit memories of being humiliated in public.
- The bulimic may experience a strong urge to binge or purge.
- Those who suffer from anger management issues may feel some level of rage.
- Those that suffer from depression may be bombarded with feelings of inadequacy.
- Those who struggle with disordered eating may be struck by a strong urge to skip meals, self-induce vomiting, or swallow laxatives.
- Those who live in poverty may be overwhelmed by thoughts of injustice or feelings of despair and hopelessness.
- And those who struggle with health issues may be struck with doubts concerning their eventual recovery.

When our feelings, images, memories, urges and triggers arise, we do not resist them—we turn to them and face them. We learn to ride out our anxiety, pain, or temptation as best we can until its strength fades. During this process, we ride out our unhealthy desires and conditioned responses just as a surfer rides the crest of a wave until it gradually dissipates and disappears.

In other words, we accept our powerlessness, and sink into the experience and reality of it without becoming lost within it. We carefully let go of our resistance to our struggle; and we move to face, accept, and embrace our struggle to the best of our abilities so that we can successfully surrender our struggle to God.

This act of surrendering our struggle to God goes against our natural instinct to fight for ourselves with weapons that we can see, feel, understand, and control. Therefore, when we surrender our battle to God, we are acting in pure faith:

> *Now faith is confidence in what we hope for and assurance about what we do not see.*
>
> **Hebrews 11:1 (*NIV*)**

We are conditioned to fight our struggles with the human weapons of denial, anger, avoidance, regression, willpower, disassociation, rationalization, isolation, projection, compartmentalization, repression, and the like. But the act of surrender requires us to: (1) put away the human weapons that we've used to fight our battles since childhood, and (2) start using the spiritual weapons of God.

> *The weapons we use are not human ones. Our weapons have power from God and can destroy the enemy's strong places.*
>
> **2 Corinthians 10:4 (*ERV*)**

When we surrender for the first time, it will be the first time we start fighting without our familiar human weapons. Fighting our struggles in this new way will feel very strange: we will feel as if we are going into battle naked because we will be trusting in weapons that we can not see! Consequently, trusting in God's weapons will feel like jumping off a cliff without first seeing the net that's there to catch you. But we take the plunge anyway, and believe that God is there to carry us to safety even when we can't actually perceive his presence with our human senses. It is this leap of faith that somehow moves God on our behalf:

> *And without faith it is impossible to please God, because anyone who comes to him must believe that he exists and that he rewards those who earnestly seek him.*
>
> **Hebrews 11:6 (*NIV*)**

In the beginning, it may be frightening to let go, and let God, but it will become easier as our confidence and faith grow in the power and reliability of our Lord and Savior. Indeed, in time, it will become less difficult to believe that we are constantly surrounded by his glory:

> *And Elisha prayed, "Open his eyes, LORD, so that he may see." Then the LORD opened the servant's eyes, and he looked and saw the hills full of horses and chariots of fire all around Elisha.*
>
> **2 Kings 6:17 (*NIV*)**

* What have you prayed for God to do for you (or for others) that God did not do?

_____

_____

_____

_____

_____

* Do you blame God for the harmful actions (such as trauma, abuse, or neglect) that others committed against you? Why or why not?

_____

_____

_____

_____

_____

* How does this affect your ability to trust in a God who allowed this to happen?

_____

_____

_____

_____

_____

* **What do you fear about surrendering your battle to God? Why?**

_____

_____

_____

_____

_____

_____

* **What experiences have caused you to lose faith in God? Why?**

_____

_____

_____

_____

_____

_____

The act of surrender requires us to learn how to climb into the loving arms of our God in the same way that many of us did as children with our mothers and fathers:

> *People were also bringing babies to Jesus for him to place his hands on them. When the disciples saw this, they rebuked them. But Jesus called the children to him and said, "Let the little children come to me, and do not hinder them, for the kingdom of God belongs to such as these. Truly I tell you, anyone who will not receive the kingdom of God like a little child will never enter it."*
>
> **Luke 18:15–17 (*NIV*)**

By surrendering, we: (1) stop resisting our struggles (such as addictions, obsessions, compulsions, temptations, or wounds) in our own strength; (2) invite God into our battle with our struggles so that he may, with our consent, break the power that our struggles have over us; and (3) wait in stillness until God answers our call for help by empowering us with the ability to endure, overcome, and resist our struggles.

* **List the areas in your life in which you do not trust God.**

_____

_____

_____

_____

_____

_____

_____

_____

* **Why do you not trust him in these areas of your life?**

_____

_____

_____

_____

_____

Our surrender actually pulls God into the deepest, scariest, and most hidden spaces of our souls. This surrender is an active demand that our God come join us in our places of pain and desperation. We believe that God will respond to our call for aid as we bring our struggles before him because we believe that our God is love:

> *Dear friends, let us love one another, for love comes from God. Everyone who loves has been born of God and knows God. Whoever does not love does not know God, because God is love. This is how God showed his love among us: he sent his one and only Son into the world that we might live through him. This is love: not that we loved God, but that he loved us and sent his Son as an atoning sacrifice for our sins.*
>
> **1 John 4:7–10 (*NIV*)**

Love is patient, love is kind. It does not envy, it does not boast, it is not proud. It does not dishonor others, it is not self-seeking, it is not easily angered, it keeps no record of wrongs. Love does not delight in evil but rejoices with the truth. It always protects, always trusts, always hopes, always perseveres. Love never fails.

1 Corinthians 13:4–8 (*NIV*)

And we believe that God has proven his love for us through his son Jesus Christ:

But God shows his love for us in that while we were still sinners, Christ died for us.

Romans 5:8 (*ESV*)

"For God so loved the world that he gave his only Son, that whoever believes in him should not perish but have eternal life."

John 3:16 (*NIV*)

(See also Luke 23:33–34.)

* **What do you still have hope for—even though you believe God has let you down?**

_____

_____

_____

_____

_____

_____

_____

* **Why do you still hope and believe?**

_____

_____

_____

_____

_____

_____

* **What things in your life cause you to believe that you should turn your will and life over to the care of God?**

_____

_____

_____

_____

_____

_____

closing prayer

Teach me how to surrender my battle to you. I am desperate to learn how to let my human weapons go so that I can pick up and begin using your divine weapons. Increase my courage and faith in you. Help me overcome the doubts and pain of my past so that I can move forward with you by my side. Help me believe that you will be there to fight my battles for me as "I let go and let God." Amen!

chapter 14

PULLING GOD INTO THE STRUGGLE

We use the Surrender Prayer to pull God into our struggle by demanding that he come to our aid. We imagine and believe in faith that: Jesus is there with us in our struggle, that he is experiencing all that we feel, think and suffer, and that he will fight our battles for us. We believe that he is partnered with us, and that he will help us carry and overcome our burden of powerlessness, shame, guilt, embarrassment, weakness, trauma, abuse, abandonment or sin. We call on God to take up our battle and defeat our enemies:

> *Lord, how many are my foes! How many rise up against me! Many are saying of me, "God will not deliver him." But you, Lord, are a shield around me, my glory, the One who lifts my head high. I call out to the Lord, and he answers me from his holy mountain. I lie down and sleep; I wake again, because the Lord sustains me. I will not fear though tens of thousands assail me on every side. <u>Arise, Lord! Deliver me, my God! Strike all my enemies on the jaw; break the teeth of the wicked. From the Lord comes deliverance.</u> May your blessing be on your people.*
>
> **Psalm 3 (*NIV*)**

I call on you, my God, for you will answer me; turn your ear to me and hear my prayer. Show me the wonders of your great love, you who save by your right hand those who take refuge in you from their foes. . . .

Rise up, Lord, confront them, bring them down; with your sword rescue me from the wicked. By your hand save me from such people, Lord, from those of this world whose reward is in this life.

Psalm 17:6–14 (*NIV*)

Awake, Lord! Why do you sleep? Rouse yourself! Do not reject us forever. Why do you hide your face and forget our misery and oppression? We are brought down to the dust; our bodies cling to the ground. Rise up and help us; rescue us because of your unfailing love.

Psalm 44:23–26 (*NIV*)

* **Is it hard for you to ask God for help? Why?**

_____

_____

_____

_____

_____

* **Has anyone in your family failed to help you in the past? How?**

_____

_____

_____

_____

_____

* **Do you believe that God will also fail to come to your aid when you call him? Why?**

_____

_____

_____

_____

We ask God to help us overcome those feelings, thoughts, experiences and compulsions that have led us to do things that we no longer want to do. And we remain persistent—Jesus, himself, had to pray three times in the Garden of Gethsemane before his prayer was answered (Mark 14:32–42). So we need to also persevere until God answers our prayers:

> *Blessed is the one who perseveres under trial because, having stood the test, that person will receive the crown of life that the Lord has promised to those who love him.*
>
> **James 1:12 (NIV)**

> *Then Jesus told his disciples a parable to show them that they should always pray and not give up. He said: "In a certain town there was a judge who neither feared God nor cared what people thought. And there was a widow in that town who kept coming to him with the plea, 'Grant me justice against my adversary.'*
>
> *"For some time he refused. But finally he said to himself, 'Even though I don't fear God or care what people think, yet because this widow keeps bothering me, I will see that she gets justice, so that she won't eventually come and attack me!'"*
>
> *And the Lord said, "Listen to what the unjust judge says. And will not God bring about justice for his chosen ones, who cry out to him day and night? Will he keep putting them off? I tell you, he will see that they get justice, and quickly. However, when the Son of Man comes, will he find faith on the earth?"*
>
> **Luke 18:1–8 (*NIV*)**

We maintain our belief that we can reach out to God, grab ahold of him, and pull him into our battle until we can actually: (1) envision his presence, (2) begin to trust that we are not alone in our struggle, and (3) believe that God is fighting and will continue to fight on our behalf. We imagine Jesus holding us and loving us through our sadness, despair, anger, regret, lust, anxiety, and pain. And we have faith that he accepts and loves us unconditionally in our battles—that he will never reject, condemn, judge or stop loving us.

* Do you truly believe that God loves and accepts you unconditionally? Why or why not?

_____

_____

_____

_____

_____

_____

We believe that when God looks at us, he doesn't see an addict, a liar, a sexual abuser, a gossip, a criminal, a disappointment, a sexist, a batterer, a racist, a cutter, or a loser. We have confidence that he understands all of our pain and all of our weakness—that nothing inside or outside of us makes us ugly, unlovable, unworthy or irredeemable—because he doesn't see what we may see when we look in the mirror.

This doesn't mean that God is blind to the pain that we cause others, or to the pain that others have caused us. We know God sees and feels the pain of humanity's most heinous sin. But we also know that he sees beyond that sin, which enables him to see all of us as children, who desperately need his love, healing, grace, mercy, and forgiveness.

As we've discussed previously, God doesn't love the way we love. Some of us may be unable to love ourselves because of what we've done. And some of us may be unable to love others because of what they've done to us. But God loves us all no matter what:

> *Jesus said, "Father, forgive them, for they do not know what they are doing."*
> **Luke 23:24 (*NIV*)**

So please take courage and persist. Pull God into your struggle. And know that God will answer your call because he loves you!

closing prayer

Dear Father, teach me how to pull you into my struggles. Help me overcome the fear that you will reject me because of what I've done, or because of what's been done to me. Arise, O God, and show yourself strong on my behalf! I can't do it alone! Hear me when I call out to you, my Lord. Don't wait. Please don't hesitate. I need you right now! Amen.

chapter 15

WAITING ON GOD

After we pull God into our struggle, we learn to wait for God to answer our call for help. Having to wait for God's help is quite understandably the last thing that any of us want to do. We all want immediate relief from our struggles—and if such relief is not immediate, we at least want God's help to arrive within an acceptably short period of time. Nevertheless, we all know that God's timetable doesn't always coincide with our own.

There's a saying within the Black church, "He may not always come when you want him—but he's always right on time." We who practice the Surrender Prayer understand that we cannot bend the will of God to fit our individual wants and needs. On the contrary, the very purpose of the Surrender Prayer is to discover how to surrender our will and lives over to the care of God.

Accordingly, we learn to wait in faith on the Lord to strengthen us:

> *But they who wait for the Lord shall renew their strength; they shall mount up with wings like eagles; they shall run and not be weary; they shall walk and not faint.*
>
> **Isaiah 40:31 (*ESV*)**

> *I believe that I shall look upon the goodness of the Lord in the land of the living! Wait for the Lord; be strong, and let your heart take courage; wait for the Lord!*
>
> **Psalm 27:13–14 (*ESV*)**

> *The Lord is good to those who wait for him, to the soul who seeks him.*
>
> **Lamentations 3:25 (*ESV*)**

We learn how to be still within the storm of our struggles. In other words, we wait in *stillness* for our God to strengthen and empower us to overcome our enemies:

> *Moses answered the people, "Do not be afraid. Stand firm and you will see the deliverance the Lord will bring you today. The Egyptians you see today you will never see again. The Lord will fight for you; you need only to be still."*
>
> **Exodus 14:13–14 (*NIV*)**

> *Be still before the Lord, all mankind, because he has roused himself from his holy dwelling.*
>
> **Zechariah 2:13 (*NIV*)**

> *He says, "Be still, and know that I am God; I will*
> *be exalted among the nations, I will be exalted in*
> *the earth."*
>   *The Lord Almighty is with us; the God of Jacob is*
> *our fortress.*
>
>   **Psalm 46:10–11 (*NIV*)**

* **Have you ever sat in stillness with God? If yes, please describe your experience. If no, please explain why you have not.**

_____

_____

_____

_____

It is said that silence is the first language of God, and that everything else is a poor translation. Consequently, we not only learn to communicate with God in silence, but we also learn to wait in *silence* for God to strengthen us in our struggles:

> *My soul, wait in silence for God only, for my hope is*
> *from him. He only is my rock and my salvation, my*
> *stronghold; I shall not be shaken. On God my salva-*
> *tion and my glory rest; the rock of my strength, my*
> *refuge is in God. Trust in him at all times, O people;*
> *Pour out your heart before him; God is a refuge for us.*
>
>   **Psalm 62:5–8 (*NASB*)**

> *This is what the Sovereign LORD, the Holy One of Israel, says: "Only in returning to me and resting in me will you be saved. In quietness and confidence is your strength."*
>
> **Isaiah 30:15 (*NLT*)**

> *And he said, "Go out and stand on the mount before the Lord." And behold, the Lord passed by, and a great and strong wind tore the mountains and broke in pieces the rocks before the Lord, but the Lord was not in the wind. And after the wind an earthquake, but the Lord was not in the earthquake. And after the earthquake a fire, but the Lord was not in the fire. And after the fire the sound of a low whisper.*
>
> **1 Kings 19:11–12 (*ESV*)**

(See also Job 6:24.)

* **Have you ever sat in silence in God's presence during prayer? Has God ever communicated with you in a "low whisper?" Have you ever communicated with God in silence? Please describe.**

_____

_____

_____

_____

_____

_____

> *And the Holy Spirit helps us in our weakness. For example, we don't know what God wants us to pray for. But the Holy Spirit prays for us with groanings that cannot be expressed in words.*
>
> **Romans 8:26 (*NLT*)**

* Have you ever experienced the Holy Spirit praying through you without words? If yes, please describe the experience.

_____

_____

_____

_____

_____

Finally, we learn to wait in *solitude* for God:

> *Very early in the morning, while it was still dark, Jesus got up, left the house and went off to a solitary place, where he prayed.*
>
> **Mark 1:35 (*NIV*)**

> *But Jesus often withdrew to lonely places and prayed.*
>
> **Luke 5:16 (*NIV*)**

> *"But you, when you pray, go into your inner room, close your door and pray to your Father who is in secret, and your Father who sees what is done in secret will reward you."*
>
> **Matthew 6:6 (*NASB*)**

(See also Luke 5:15–16 and John 14:13.)

The end result of our surrender should be a lightening of our load. The end result of our Prayer should be an entering into his rest:

> *"Come to me, all you who are weary and burdened, and I will give you rest. Take my yoke upon you and learn from me, for I am gentle and humble in heart, and you will find rest for your souls. For my yoke is easy and my burden is light."*
>
> **Matthew 11:28–30 (*NIV*)**

Waiting in faith for God's deliverance requires us to have "confidence in what we hope for and assurance about what we do not see." (Hebrews 11:1) There will be times during the Prayer when you do not feel God's presence, protection, love, power or forgiveness. Just as Jesus cried out: "My God, my God, why have you forsaken me?"—there will be occasions when you will feel deserted by God.

However, please remember that faith is not about what we feel, but about what we believe. When we pray, we believe that God hears and answers our prayers even when we do not feel him. To the best of our individual abilities, we remain faithful and persistent in our prayers (Colossians 4:2).

> *"Therefore I tell you, whatever you ask for in prayer, believe that you have received it, and it will be yours."*
>
> **Mark 11:24 (*NIV*)**

> *And we are confident that he hears us whenever we ask for anything that pleases him. And since we know he hears us when we make our requests, we also know that he will give us what we ask for.*
>
> **1 John 5:14–15 (*NLT*)**

> *"Let us acknowledge the LORD; let us press on to acknowledge him. As surely as the sun rises, he will appear; he will come to us like the winter rains, like the spring rains that water the earth."*
>
> **Hosea 6:3 (*NIV*)**

Our situations and circumstances may not change. Our battles, struggles, and conflicts may still remain. But we now have the tools to help us overcome them for one day, one hour, one minute—and if need be—one second at a time. We can now develop the ability to turn to God instead of turning to our destructive coping mechanisms and self-medicating behaviors to help us find peace, relief, and rest from our addictions, fears, sadness and temptations.

closing prayer

Dear God, I need your help right now. And I definitely don't want to wait for it. But you have shown me time and time again that I don't get to decide when or how your help comes. God, teach me how to wait on you. Give me the understanding, patience, faith, and endurance to wait in stillness, silence, and solitude for your help in the storm of my struggles. And as I wait for you, I need you to give me the strength to persevere when I don't feel your presence, love, acceptance, or forgiveness. Allow me to enter your rest as I pray to you. Let me experience your peace, which transcends all understanding, as I wait on you. But please don't make me wait too long, God, because I need you right now. Amen.

chapter 16

JESUS IN THE GARDEN

The Surrender Prayer helps reveal the link between God's love, and the suffering that both Jesus and we endure as an inescapable aspect of our human condition. Too many mainstream churches spend a great deal of time teaching us how Jesus carried his own cross to Golgotha to be crucified, but often fail to teach each of us how to carry our own individual crosses. If we are true followers of our Lord and Savior Jesus Christ, all of us in our own individual ways can follow the example of Jesus:

> *Then Jesus told his disciples, "If anyone would come after me, let him deny himself and take up his cross and follow me. For whoever would save his life will lose it, but whoever loses his life for my sake will find it. For what will it profit a man if he gains the whole world and forfeits his soul? Or what shall a man give in return for his soul?"*
> **Matthew 16:24–26 (ESV)**

Jesus didn't carry his cross to abrogate our responsibility of carrying our own cross: Jesus carried his cross to *show us how* to carry our own. When we carry our own cross, we are actively striving to live our lives surrendered to the will of God—even when the will of God runs contrary to our own will. We fortunately serve a God of mercy and grace who knows that we do not have the necessary internal resources to live our lives in accordance with his will without his help. Consequently, our ability to carry our cross effectively is completely dependent upon God empowering us to do so. And God's ability to empower us is completely dependent upon our willingness to allow him to do so.

* **What cross are you not carrying? How are you not living your life in accordance with God's will?**

_____

_____

_____

_____

_____

_____

* **In what ways have you rejected God's will for your life? Why?**

_____

_____

_____

_____

_____

* **What have been the consequences of such rejection?**

_____

_____

_____

_____

_____

_____

The Garden of Gethsemane represents the definitive example of how we can strive to become strengthened with God's Spirit so that we can carry our own cross:

> *On reaching the place, he said to them, "Pray that you will not fall into temptation." He withdrew about a stone's throw beyond them, knelt down and prayed, "Father, if you are willing, take this cup from me; yet not my will, but yours be done." An angel from heaven appeared to him and strengthened him. And being in anguish, he prayed more earnestly, and his sweat was like drops of blood falling to the ground.*
>
> *When he rose from prayer and went back to the disciples, he found them asleep, exhausted from sorrow. "Why are you sleeping?" he asked them. "Get up and pray so that you will not fall into temptation."*
>
> **Luke 22:40–46 (NIV)**

* Have you ever previously tried to discern God's will for your life? What did you discern?

_____

_____

_____

_____

_____

_____

* Are there any areas of struggle that you have discovered you do not whole-heartedly want God to remove even though you know these struggles are hurting you and others around you? Please explain.

_____

_____

_____

_____

_____

_____

_____

Jesus in the garden is the perfect model of surrender. Jesus went to the garden fully aware of the struggle that was raging inside of him. He knew that there was a part of himself that wanted to fulfill God's plan, but also a part of himself that did not. Jesus did not run away from this internal conflict, but chose to accept it. Jesus sat with his fear, pain, and despair; and was able to get real with his Father. He shared his true feelings with God, and confessed that he didn't want to go to the cross—but Jesus did not use his own power or authority to save himself:

> *"Do you think I cannot call on my Father, and he will at once put at my disposal more than twelve legions of angels?"*
>
> **Matthew 26:53 (NIV)**

Jesus did not act outside of God's will because He recognized that he could accomplish nothing apart from his Father's will:

> *"I can do nothing on my own. As I hear, I judge, and my judgment is just, because I seek not my own will but the will of him who sent me."*
>
> **John 5:30 (ESV)**

> *"Very truly I tell you, the Son can do nothing by himself; he can do only what he sees his Father doing, because whatever the Father does the Son also does."*
>
> **John 5:19 (NIV)**

Instead, Jesus surrendered his will to his Father in heaven:

> *"Father, if you are willing, take this cup from me; yet not my will, but yours be done."*
>
> **Luke 22:42 (*NIV*)**

* Jesus trusted his Father's will for his life. What hinders your ability to trust God?

_____

_____

_____

_____

_____

_____

_____

* When has trusting in God failed you? How?

_____

_____

_____

_____

_____

_____

_____

* **How has trusting in your own understanding, feelings, or emotions gotten you in trouble?**

_____

_____

_____

_____

_____

* **When has trusting in other people failed you?**

_____

_____

_____

_____

_____

But his surrender wasn't easy! Even Jesus had to be strengthened by God before he could completely surrender his will to God in prayer:

> *An angel from heaven appeared to him and strengthened him.*
>
> **Luke 22:43 (*NIV*)**

> *And being in anguish, he prayed more earnestly, and his sweat was like drops of blood falling to the ground.*
>
> **Luke 22:44 (*NIV*)**

So if Jesus struggled with his surrender, how much more will we struggle with our surrender? We, just like Jesus, need to be strengthened by God to surrender our wills. This realization of our utter dependence upon God is the key to understanding what surrender really is: our acknowledgement that we can accomplish nothing without him.

> *"I am the vine; you are the branches. If you remain in me and I in you, you will bear much fruit; apart from me you can do nothing."*
>
> **John 15:5 (*NIV*)**

It is the admission of our powerlessness in our struggles that paradoxically allows God to begin empowering us as believers to overcome our struggles. When we sincerely tell God that we don't want to keep "doing it our way"—but his way instead—we turn over our will to God; and begin tapping into his power just as Jesus did in the garden. By surrendering his will to God, Jesus transformed the anguish and despair that he felt in the garden into a newfound strength, courage and eagerness to fulfill his destiny once he left the garden:

> *"Behold, the hour is at hand and the Son of Man is being betrayed into the hands of sinners. Get up, let us be going; behold, the one who betrays Me is at hand!"*
>
> **Matthew 26:45–46 (*NASB*)**

Consequently, we are eternally grateful that Jesus was strengthened by his surrender to God because his surrender led to the redemption of all humanity:

> *When he had received the drink, Jesus said, "It is finished." With that, he bowed his head and gave up his spirit.*
>
> **John 19:30 (*NIV*)**

When Jesus surrendered his will to God's will, Jesus provided the ultimate evidence of his and God's love for all of us:

> *"Greater love has no one than this: to lay down one's life for one's friends."*
>
> **John 15:13 (*NIV*)**

* **What do you fear losing if you turn your life and will over completely to God?**

_____

_____

_____

_____

_____

_____

_____

* **What's the worst thing that could happen?**

_____

_____

_____

_____

_____

_____

_____

* **What fears surface when you think of trusting God for your future instead of trusting yourself?**

_____

_____

_____

_____

_____

_____

_____

* **Do you believe that God's will is best for you? Why or why not?**

_____

_____

_____

_____

_____

_____

_____

_____

The path of surrender that Jesus chose activated God's movement to save the world. Jesus was only able to make this ultimate sacrifice because he willingly turned over his will and life to God beforehand. This voluntary surrender enabled Jesus to: (1) be strengthened by God to overcome this final struggle, (2) fulfill the mission for which he was sent, and (3) ultimately sit at the right hand of God (Acts 7:55–56). Accordingly, it is through our struggles that we can also initiate God's movement in our lives (as well as in the lives of others) if we choose to surrender in our own struggles.

When we struggle, we can voluntarily surrender our sin, pain, craving, wound, oppression, trauma, depression, anxiety or addiction to God, and become empowered by his Spirit; or we can continue to resort to our own ultimately ineffective coping mechanisms, self-medicating behaviors and survival skills, which will never enable us to achieve victory in Christ. As the 12-Steppers say: "Insanity is doing the same thing over and over again, but expecting different results."

Through our surrender, we strive never to return to our old, ineffective and destructive self-medicating behaviors. The Prayer helps us surrender in our struggles so that we may access the power of God to help us overcome our struggles. Within this surrender lies the key to our own victory and blessings in Jesus. We access the same power source that allowed Jesus to be victorious at the cross, which resulted in his ultimate blessing:

Who, being in very nature God, did not consider equality with God something to be used to his own advantage; rather, he made himself nothing by taking the very nature of a servant, being made in human likeness.

And being found in appearance as a man, he humbled himself by becoming obedient to death—even death on a cross!

Therefore God exalted him to the highest place and gave him the name that is above every name, that at the name of Jesus every knee should bow, in heaven and on earth and under the earth, and every tongue acknowledge that Jesus Christ is Lord, to the glory of God the Father.

Philippians 2:5–11 (*NIV*)

closing prayer

Dear God, I want to be like Jesus in the Garden, but I need you to show me how. Putting my life completely in your hands scares me. It's not easy letting you take control when I want to do it my way. Help me learn how to place my trust in you. Give me the faith to believe that your will for me is always what's best for me in the end. Amen!

chapter 17

BLESSINGS IN THE STRUGGLE

While it is undeniably clear that Jesus was blessed through his suffering at the cross, many of us still do not equate God's blessings with our own personal struggles. We do not view suffering Christians as blessed. On the contrary, we believe that the absence of suffering in our lives is the hallmark of being blessed by God. The Bible turns this belief on its head:

> *More than that, we rejoice in our sufferings, knowing that suffering produces endurance, and endurance produces character, and character produces hope, and hope does not put us to shame, because God's love has been poured into our hearts through the Holy Spirit who has been given to us.*
> **Romans 5:3–5 (ESVUK)**

> *And after you have suffered a little while, the God of all grace, who has called you to his eternal glory in Christ, will himself restore, confirm, strengthen, and establish you.*
> **1 Peter 5:10 (ESV)**

> *Dear brothers and sisters, when troubles come your way, consider it an opportunity for great joy. For you know that when your faith is tested, your endurance has a chance to grow. So let it grow, for when your endurance is fully developed, you will be perfect and complete, needing nothing.*
>
> **James 1:2–4 (*NLT*)**

(See also Romans 8:18, Luke 14:27, Philippians 1:29, Psalm 34:19, 2 Corinthians 4:8–10, and 2 Timothy 3:12.)

Through the blessing of suffering, we are transformed more and more into the likeness of Jesus:

> *But whatever were gains to me I now consider loss for the sake of Christ. What is more, I consider everything a loss because of the surpassing worth of knowing Christ Jesus my Lord, for whose sake I have lost all things. I consider them garbage, that I may gain Christ and be found in him, not having a righteousness of my own that comes from the law, but that which is through faith in Christ—the righteousness that comes from God on the basis of faith. I want to know Christ—yes, to know the power of his resurrection and participation in his sufferings, becoming like him in his death, and so, somehow, attaining to the resurrection from the dead.*
>
> **Philippians 3:7–11 (*NIV*)**

We think that Christians who possess wealth, power, or prestige are "blessed." This outlook, however, is inconsistent with the New Testament and many parts of the Old Testament:

> *"Blessed are you who are poor, for yours is the kingdom of God. Blessed are you who hunger now, for you will be satisfied. Blessed are you who weep now, for you will laugh."*
>
> **Luke 6:20–21 (*NIV*)**

> *Remember, dear brothers and sisters, that few of you were wise in the world's eyes or powerful or wealthy when God called you. Instead, God chose things the world considers foolish in order to shame those who think they are wise. And he chose things that are powerless to shame those who are powerful. God chose things despised by the world, things counted as nothing at all, and used them to bring to nothing what the world considers important. As a result, no one can ever boast in the presence of God.*
>
> **1 Corinthians 1:26–29 (*NLT*)**

> *But the LORD said to Samuel, "Do not consider his appearance or his height, for I have rejected him. The LORD does not look at the things people look at. People look at the outward appearance, but the LORD looks at the heart."*
>
> **1 Samuel 16:7 (*NIV*)**

(See also 1 John 2:15–17, 1 Timothy 6:9–10, Hebrews 13:5, James 2:1–7, James 5:1–6, Acts 2:44–45, Matthew 19:21–24, Luke 6:24, Luke 16:13, Matthew 6:19, 2 Corinthians 8:9, Luke 12:33, Ecclesiastes 5:10–12, Matthew 6:24, James 4:4–10, Matthew 6:19–21, 1 Timothy 6:17–19, Proverbs 30:8–9, Luke 12:15, Proverbs 23:4–5, Proverbs 15:16, Psalm 37:16, Proverbs 28:6 and Jeremiah 9:23–24.)

Many of us are in desperate need of a shift in perspective of what we believe God's blessings to be. The Prayer reminds us that the pain, struggles, and wounds we experience are not the result of a God who fails to bless or love us, but, instead, the result of a God who allows us to experience the struggles of life with the hope that we will eventually seek him out in our pain. If given the opportunity through our surrender to him, God will use every harmful event in our lives (no matter how horrendous) to draw us closer to him in order for our healing to take place:

> *And we know that in all things God works for the good of those who love him, who have been called according to his purpose.*
>
> **Romans 8:28 (NIV)**

Our struggles with low self-esteem, anxiety, sexism, abuse, abandonment, and any and all other issues have given us a lifetime of pain. God is calling out to us through our pain: he wants to use our battle with our struggles as a means to build a stronger relationship with us. In a sense, God has been waiting patiently for us to find him in our troubles, wounds, trauma and heartache. Accordingly, the Prayer is one method to help us access God in our struggles so that we can discover how to stop depending upon our old, destructive patterns of behavior and begin experiencing the healing power of our Lord and Savior.

* Which struggles (such as wounds, sins, addictions, resentments, or obsessions) are you not ready to have God remove? What are you not willing to let go of? Why?

_____

_____

_____

_____

_____

_____

_____

_____

* Why are you still attached to such struggles?

_____

_____

_____

_____

_____

_____

_____

* **What do you fear will happen if God removes your struggles?**

We who wrestle daily with the pain of our struggles may at times believe that we have been cursed by God (or some other supernatural entity), but the divine healing that God can provide us has the power to transform our curses into blessings. God did it for Jesus; Christ has done it for all of us:

> *But Christ has bought us out from under the doom of that impossible system by taking the curse for our wrongdoing upon himself. For it is written in the Scripture, "Anyone who is hanged on a tree is cursed" (as Jesus was hung upon a wooden cross). Now God can bless the Gentiles, too, with this same blessing he promised to Abraham; and all of us as Christians can have the promised Holy Spirit through this faith.*
>
> **Galatians 3:13–14 (TLB)**

If we surrender our "curses" to God in faith, God will transform them into blessings. Accordingly, our struggles are opportunities for transformation, but our struggles remain curses if we do not allow the Holy Spirit to dwell within us:

> *Guard, through the Holy Spirit who dwells in us, the treasure, which has been entrusted to you.*
>
> **2 Timothy 1:14 (*NASB*)**

Our struggles are transformed into blessings when our wounds are transformed into sacred wounds. Our wounds become sacred wounds when our wounds no longer compel us to harm others, or ourselves but, instead, draw us closer to God, and become the channel through which the fruit of the Holy Spirit flows:

> *But when the Holy Spirit controls our lives he will produce this kind of fruit in us: love, joy, peace, patience, kindness, goodness, faithfulness, gentleness and self-control; and here there is no conflict with Jewish laws.*
>
> **Galatians 5:22–23 (*TLB*)**

We will know that the Holy Spirit is changing us when the wounds of our struggles no longer have the power to overwhelm us. When we no longer have to get high on alcohol or drugs; abuse others or ourselves; masturbate to pornography; commit criminal acts to survive or to escape the daily pain of our emotional wounds; cut ourselves; be workaholics; binge or purge; go to strip clubs and massage parlors; become addicted to exercise, videogames, or Facebook; exploit or manipulate others; gamble; or be codependent upon others; we will know that we are no longer slaves to our struggles.

closing prayer

Dear God, I want to believe that my current struggles will somehow be transformed into future spiritual blessings! Please help me trust that you will carry and bless me through my life's trials. I want to believe that you can and will transform my painful wounds into sacred wounds. Please give me the faith and strength to follow you in surrender each morning that I wake. Thank you, Jesus. Amen!

chapter 18

THE POWER OF CHOICE, TEMPTATION, AND GOD'S GRACE

As children of God, we no longer have to be slaves to our sins, or to any other struggle we encounter. Whether we believe it or not, God has already set us free from the chains that bind us:

> *It was for freedom that Christ set us free; therefore keep standing firm and do not be subject again to a yoke of slavery.*
>
> **Galatians 5:1 (*NASB*)**

> *So you have not received a spirit that makes you fearful slaves. Instead, you received God's Spirit when he adopted you as his own children. Now we call him, "Abba, Father."*
>
> **Romans 8:15 (*NLT*)**

Therefore do not let sin reign in your mortal body so that you obey its lusts, and do not go on presenting the members of your body to sin as instruments of unrighteousness; but present yourselves to God as those alive from the dead, and your members as instruments of righteousness to God. For sin shall not be master over you, for you are not under law but under grace.

What then? Shall we sin because we are not under law but under grace? May it never be! Do you not know that when you present yourselves to someone as slaves for obedience, you are slaves of the one whom you obey, either of sin resulting in death, or of obedience resulting in righteousness? But thanks be to God that though you were slaves of sin, you became obedient from the heart to that form of teaching to which you were committed, and having been freed from sin, you became slaves of righteousness.

Romans 6:12–18 (*NASB*)

(See also Jeremiah 29:11–14 and Hebrews 2:14–15.)

Our surrender empowers us with the ability to make a choice of whom we shall follow. When we were slaves to our struggles, we were slaves to our destructive behaviors, thoughts and feelings—we had no choice but to act out our hurtful obsessions and compulsions. Now, we have the divine gift of choice.

"But if serving the LORD seems undesirable to you, then choose for yourselves this day whom you will serve, whether the gods your ancestors served beyond the Euphrates, or the gods of the Amorites, in whose land you are living. But as for me and my household, we will serve the LORD."

Joshua 24:15 (*NIV*)

"Today I have given you the choice between life and death, between blessings and curses. Now I call on heaven and earth to witness the choice you make. Oh, that you would choose life, so that you and your descendants might live!"

Deuteronomy 30:19 (*NLT*)

* What has "enslaved" you in the past?

_____

_____

_____

_____

_____

_____

God has done his part to set us free, but we still have to do our part. On each and every day of our lives, we all have to choose whom we will follow. Our power of choice to choose freedom in Christ is dependent upon a daily surrender to our Lord and Savior. This component of free will means that we can still choose to become fearful slaves again. God will never make our choice to follow him for us, but he will help us in our struggles if we use our free will to follow him.

As stated, we did not have the power to choose God's way when we were under the yoke of slavery. The power to resist temptation and to choose to surrender our struggles to God is a gift from him. Nevertheless, there will always be a part of us that will be tempted not to follow God's will. God allows these temptations to remain because he wants only willing participants to be a part of his family. If he were to remove all of our temptations, we would no longer be willing participants—but robots instead. This means that we can access the power of God to overcome our temptations only if we first choose to surrender our will to him just as Jesus did in the garden.

Please realize that we are not sinning or acting against God's will when we are tempted. The Bible is very clear on this point. In fact, Jesus, whom we believe was without sin, was tempted far more often and in far more ways than we will ever be tempted:

> *For we do not have a high priest who is unable to empathize with our weaknesses, but we have one who has been tempted in every way, just as we are— yet he did not sin.*
>
> **Hebrews 4:15 (NIV)**

However, unlike Jesus, many of our temptations have resulted in sin. Thank God, we have a loving, understanding and accepting Father who has given us all the gift of grace.

As we've previously discussed, to struggle as a Christian is normal and to be expected. For many of us, our daily struggle is a fight to resist the temptation to sin. If this is your struggle, you have undoubtedly asked God countless times to release you from such temptation—and have probably been saddened, frustrated or angered by the fact that God has not answered your prayers. You are not alone in your disappointment with God's reply:

> *Therefore, in order to keep me from becoming conceited, I was given a thorn in my flesh, a messenger of Satan, to torment me. Three times I pleaded with the Lord to take it away from me. But he said to me, "My grace is sufficient for you, for my power is made perfect in weakness." Therefore I will boast all the more gladly about my weaknesses, so that Christ's power may rest on me. That is why, for Christ's sake, I delight in weaknesses, in insults, in hardships, in persecutions, in difficulties. For when I am weak, then I am strong.*
>
> **2 Corinthians 12:7–10 (*NIV*)**

Paul asked God three times to remove the thorn in his flesh. And God replied: "My grace is sufficient for you, for my power is made perfect in weakness." The Merriam-Webster Dictionary defines grace as: "the unmerited divine assistance given humans for their regeneration or sanctification." We define grace as God's freely given and unconditional promise to love, accept, forgive and empower us in our pain, weakness, powerlessness, failure and sin as we strive to draw closer to him.

Regardless of what we do (and how many times we do it), God's grace is sufficient to see us through our struggles. Please remember that it is the acknowledgment and acceptance of our weakness, and our utter dependence upon our loving God that allows his power to begin flowing through us. God has given us this amazing grace because he knows that we will always fall far short of living in perfect accordance with his will.

Nevertheless, his grace is not to be used as a get out of jail free card:

> *Don't be misled; remember that you can't ignore God and get away with it: a man will always reap just the kind of crop he sows! If he sows to please his own wrong desires, he will be planting seeds of evil and he will surely reap a harvest of spiritual decay and death; but if he plants the good things of the Spirit, he will reap the everlasting life that the Holy Spirit gives him.*
>
> **Galatians 6:7–8 (*TLB*)**

> *Dear friends, if we deliberately continue sinning after we have received knowledge of the truth, there is no longer any sacrifice that will cover these sins.*
>
> **Hebrews 10:26 (*NLT*)**

While God accepts and loves us for all that we are, he certainly does not approve of all that we do. God neither spoils, nor enables his children, which means that he allows us to reap the consequences of our actions to help teach us right from wrong.

* **How have you used God's grace as a get out of jail free card in the past?**

_____

_____

_____

_____

_____

_____

_____

In summary, the key concept to remember is this: when we fall into temptation and sin, his grace is always sufficient to lift us back up again. As Donnie McClurkin sings in his song entitled "We Fall Down":

> *We fall down*
> *but we get up.*
> *We fall down*
> *but we get up.*
> *We fall down*
> *but we get up.*
> *For a saint*
> *is just a sinner who fell down,*
> *but we couldn't stay there,*
> *and got up!*

closing prayer

Please sing this well-known hymn to the Lord as your prayer:

> *Amazing grace, how sweet the sound*
> *that saved a wretch like me.*
> *I once was lost, but now I am found,*
> *was blind, but now I see.*

'Twas grace that taught my heart to fear,
and grace my fears relieved.
How precious did that grace appear
the hour I first believed.

Through many dangers, toils and snares
I have already come,
'tis grace has brought me safe thus far
and grace will lead me home.

The Lord has promised good to me
His word my hope secures;
He will my shield and portion be,
as long as life endures.

Yea, when this flesh and heart shall fail,
and mortal life shall cease
I shall possess within the veil,
a life of joy and peace.

When we've been there ten thousand years
bright shining as the sun,
we've no less days to sing God's praise
than when we've first begun.

Amen. Thank you, Jesus…

chapter 19

WHY AM I STILL STRUGGLING WITH THIS?

> *Then he said to all, "Anyone who wants to follow me must put aside his own desire and conveniences and carry his cross with him every day and keep close to me! Whoever loses his life for my sake will save it, but whoever insists on keeping his life will lose it; and what profit is there in gaining the whole world when it means forfeiting one's self?"*
>
> **Luke 9:23–25 (*TLB*)**

Christianity is not a spectator sport—nor is it for the faint of heart. If we choose to follow Jesus, we are choosing to carry our cross just as Jesus carried his cross on the road to Calvary. The cross that we carry is the struggle that we surrender to God in prayer each and every day. This cross represents our daily decision to turn our will and our lives over to the care of God.

There was no shortcut on the road to Calvary for Jesus, but it is human nature to expect, or hope for, a shortcut in our own personal Christian walk. Many of us were told that we would be miraculously released from our struggles if we did one or more of the following:

- prayed the "right" way,
- tried hard enough to live the "right" way,
- had the "right" Church leader lay hands on us,
- attended the "right" number of prayer meetings or weekly small groups,
- read the "right" Christian books,
- listened to the "right" pastor,
- attended the "right" church,
- possessed the "right" amount of faith,
- joined the "right" church ministry,
- purchased the "right" Christian sermon videos and tapes,
- tithed the "right" amount each week,
- volunteered the "right" number of hours of our personal time to help others in need, or
- participated in the "right" Christian convention, revival, retreat or conference.

While this guidance may have worked for those who offered such advice, this counsel has not worked for those of us who have discovered that some struggles remain no matter what we do.

* **If God told you today that he will never completely remove your struggle(s) from your life, what would your response be?**

_____

_____

_____

_____

_____

_____

_____

_____

_____

_____

We have all prayed innumerable times for God to remove our struggles. And we have probably all at some point doubted our salvation, and God's existence, love, or power, when he has not answered our prayers by removing struggles from our lives.

God in his power can certainly free us from our battles with temptation and suffering. For example, God could heal our minds and bodies so that we are never again tempted, or triggered, to relapse into old destructive addictions, obsessions or compulsions. But while we who practice the Surrender Prayer always hope for such divine and absolute deliverance, we understand that such liberation is more often the exception than the rule. We believe that our suffering in the struggle is what drew us to God in the first place, and what maintains our daily dependence upon him. In other words, we believe that the complete elimination of the temptation, craving or urge to return to our old, destructive ways of living would inevitably lead us to slowly fade away from our commitment, relationship, dependence and surrender to God.

We all have built-in forgetters that constantly try to sabotage our awareness and acceptance of the fact that only our daily surrender and dependence upon God give us power to overcome our struggles. Consequently, we need reminders of our powerlessness so that we do not forget that it was God who transformed our curses into blessings, and our wounds into sacred wounds:

One of the twelve disciples, Thomas (nicknamed the Twin), was not with the others when Jesus came. They told him, "We have seen the Lord!"

But he replied, "I won't believe it unless I see the nail wounds in his hands, put my fingers into them, and place my hand into the wound in his side."

Eight days later the disciples were together again, and this time Thomas was with them. The doors were locked; but suddenly, as before, Jesus was standing among them. "Peace be with you," he said. Then he said to Thomas, "Put your finger here, and look at my hands. Put your hand into the wound in my side. Don't be faithless any longer. Believe!"

"My Lord and my God!" Thomas exclaimed.

John 20:24–28 (*NLT*)

Just as Thomas needed to see and touch the sacred wounds of Jesus to believe that God raised Jesus from the dead, we need to perceive our own wounds on a daily basis so that we never forget what our God has done for us. Our reminders are often the temptations, cravings and triggers that will still pursue us at times—even after we have been empowered by the Holy Spirit to successfully thwart their attacks. Please remember that our surrender to God is not a one-shot deal: it is a daily practice.

"'Our Father in heaven, hallowed be your name, your kingdom come, your will be done, on earth as it is in heaven. Give us today our daily bread. And forgive us our debts, as we also have forgiven our debtors. And lead us not into temptation, but deliver us from the evil one.'"

Matthew 6:9–13 (*NIV*)

God in his wisdom may intentionally leave a thorn in our flesh so that we will learn to seek, trust and depend upon him each morning just as the Jews did in the desert long ago:

> *Then the Lord said to Moses, "I will rain down bread from heaven for you. <u>The people are to go out each day and gather enough for that day.</u> In this way I will test them and see whether they will follow my instructions."*
>
> **Exodus 16:4 (*NIV*)**

True recovery, or deliverance, from our struggles doesn't make our desire to do something that is harmful to ourselves and to others disappear. True recovery is the gift of our daily bread, which enables us to live one day at a time in victory over the struggles that we encounter. When we awaken each morning, we are confronted with a choice: we can choose again to be a slave to our struggles and continue destroying ourselves, or we can surrender to God and allow him to love, empower, transform, and bless us.

* **If God removed your thorns, what, if any, long-term effect would it have on your relationship with him?**

_____

_____

_____

_____

_____

Our current circumstances and situations may not change, but the evidence of God's movement in our lives is our ability to withstand the onslaught of our struggles for the first time without resorting to our own destructive obsessions and compulsions to escape or numb out our pain. A daily Surrender Prayer practice will lead to a daily lightening of our burden. We will experience a release and relief from our struggles one day at a time. We will gain a greater level of confidence and trust (not in ourselves but in the power and ability of our God to help us) as the Holy Spirit grants us the power to resist the temptations of our battles, and provides us with an ever-increasing reservoir of his fruit while we continue to fight our struggles in God's strength:

> *But when the Holy Spirit controls our lives he will produce this kind of fruit in us: love, joy, peace, patience, kindness, goodness, faithfulness, gentleness and self-control; and here there is no conflict with Jewish laws.*
>
> **Galatians 5:22–23 (TLB)**

For example, the drug addict will learn to overcome her craving to use drugs, and will be able to access (perhaps for the first time in her life) the peace of God. The sex addict will learn to resist the temptation to seek out a prostitute, and will be able to experience a level of self-control that he has never before felt. A woman who suffers from depression will learn to resist her self-condemning thoughts of worthlessness, and will feel the love of

God. And the man who struggles with anger issues will learn to resist the urge to lash out in rage at his children, and will become capable of expressing himself with gentleness.

The Surrender Prayer does not promise us a quick fix. Hard work, self-discipline, dedication, desperation, the awareness and acceptance of our powerlessness, and a daily surrender to God are all necessary prerequisites to allow God to begin changing us from the inside out. The changes that we desire may not happen overnight, but if we believe in the word of God, and have faith and hope in what he has promised us as his children, the victory will be ours. In fact, although, we may not feel very victorious at times, the victory has been guaranteed for those of us who believe!

> *"I have told you these things, so that in me you may have peace. In this world you will have trouble. But take heart! I have overcome the world."*
>
> **John 16:33 (NIV)**

> *But thanks be to God! He gives us the victory through our Lord Jesus Christ.*
>
> **1 Corinthians 15:57 (NIV)**

Please note that while the surrender of our struggles to God is an indispensible part of our walk with Jesus, it is only the starting point of our journey with him. Our relationship with God will be marked by an ever-increasing surrender of all aspects of our lives to him as our relationship with him grows in trust, hope, faith and love. God's ultimate call for us all is not just the surrender of our addictions, wounds, traumas, battles and pain to him, but, as the Third Step of AA asserts, the surrender of our will and our very lives to him. We, Christians, necessarily believe that the very purpose of our existence lies within the surrender of everything that we are to our God who loves us more than we could ever comprehend or imagine:

> *And so, dear brothers and sisters, I plead with you to give your bodies to God because of all he has done for you. Let them be a living and holy sacrifice—the kind he will find acceptable. This is truly the way to worship him. Don't copy the behavior and customs of this world, but let God transform you into a new person by changing the way you think. Then you will learn to know God's will for you, which is good and pleasing and perfect.*
>
> **Romans 12:1–2 (*NLT*)**

> *I have been crucified with Christ: and I myself no longer live, but Christ lives in me. And the real life I now have within this body is a result of my trusting in the Son of God, who loved me and gave himself for me.*
>
> **Galatians 2:20 (*TLB*)**

closing prayer

Jesus, I believe you know me better than I know myself. So I'm going to be as real and honest with you as I can right now. I pray and hope that you will remove my struggles from me. I have so much pain, anger, fear and sadness inside of me because of what I've been through. I admit that I have blamed you for the things that have gone wrong in my life. I even admit that there might be a part of me that resents you right now for the struggles that I battle everyday. But if you choose not to remove my struggles, please help me to submit to God's will just as you did in the garden. Please give me the strength and courage to persevere. Please show me that you still love me, even though, I have to continue dealing with this pain. Please give me the faith to believe that you will use my struggles to draw me closer to you! And please don't let all my tears be in vain! Amen.

chapter 20

WELCOMING AND EMBRACING THE STRUGGLE

At the deepest level of surrender to God, we move past our need for him to remove our struggles, and progress to such a profound level of faith and trust in him that we learn to actually welcome and embrace our struggles. The Apostle James discussed this level of surrender. Three different translations have been provided for your reflection:

> *Consider it pure joy, my brothers and sisters, when-ever you face trials of many kinds, because you know that the testing of your faith produces perseverance. Let perseverance finish its work so that you may be mature and complete, not lacking anything.*
>
> **James 1:2–4 (*NIV*)**

> *Consider it a sheer gift, friends, when tests and challenges come at you from all sides. You know that under pressure, your faith-life is forced into the open and shows its true colors. So don't try to get out of anything prematurely. Let it do its work so you become mature and well-developed, not deficient in any way.*
>
> **James 1:2–4 (MSG)**

> *Dear brothers, is your life full of difficulties and temptations? Then be happy, for when the way is rough, your patience has a chance to grow. So let it grow, and don't try to squirm out of your problems. For when your patience is finally in full bloom, then you will be ready for anything, strong in character, full and complete.*
>
> **James 1:2–4 (TLB)**

* Do you believe embracing your struggles to be a calling that you could never fulfill?

_____

_____

_____

_____

_____

_____

* **List the reasons why it would be so difficult to embrace and welcome your struggles.**

_____

_____

_____

_____

_____

It is only through the power of the Holy Spirit that we may learn to welcome, make peace with and ultimately embrace our struggles. And it is only through the wisdom of the Holy Spirit that we can learn to see our struggles as pathways to God's love, power, and healing.

> *And we know that in all things God works for the good of those who love him, who have been called according to his purpose.*
>
> **Romans 8:28 (*NIV*)**

* **Do you believe that drawing closer to God may someday require you to embrace and welcome your struggles? Why or why not?**

_____

_____

_____

_____

Like the Apostle James, we believe the Apostle Paul lived his life at an equivalent level of surrender to God:

They say they serve Christ? But I have served him far more! (Have I gone mad to boast like this?) I have worked harder, been put in jail more often, been whipped times without number, and faced death again and again and again. Five different times the Jews gave me their terrible thirty-nine lashes. Three times I was beaten with rods. Once I was stoned. Three times I was shipwrecked. Once I was in the open sea all night and the whole next day. I have traveled many weary miles and have been often in great danger from flooded rivers and from robbers and from my own people, the Jews, as well as from the hands of the Gentiles. I have faced grave dangers from mobs in the cities and from death in the deserts and in the stormy seas and from men who claim to be brothers in Christ but are not. I have lived with weariness and pain and sleepless nights. Often I have been hungry and thirsty and have gone without food; often I have shivered with cold, without enough clothing to keep me warm.

Then, besides all this, I have the constant worry of how the churches are getting along: Who makes a mistake and I do not feel his sadness? Who falls without my longing to help him? Who is spiritually hurt without my fury rising against the one who hurt him?

But if I must brag, I would rather brag about the things that show how weak I am. God, the Father of our Lord Jesus Christ, who is to be praised forever and ever, knows I tell the truth.

2 Corinthians 11:23–31 (TLB)

* **What feelings do you experience when you think about embracing and welcoming your struggles?**

_____

_____

_____

_____

_____

Through his absolute surrender to God, Paul was able to tap into the power of the Holy Spirit to overcome all the trials he faced on his journey to spread the Gospel around the world:

> *Not that I was ever in need, for I have learned how to be content with whatever I have. I know how to live on almost nothing or with everything. I have learned the secret of living in every situation, whether it is with a full stomach or empty, with plenty or little. For I can do everything through Christ, who gives me strength.*
>
> **Philippians 4:11–13 (NLT)**

The vast majority of us will never endure the intense hardships that the Apostle Paul endured. But we can recognize that even under the worst circumstances of life, God will be there in our hardships waiting for us to call out to him.

We are not masochists, but we recognize that certain struggles may persist indefinitely. We also recognize that we are closest to God when we surrender all to him in our struggles. Nevertheless, we never stop hoping and praying that God will someday free us from our daily battles.

The Surrender Prayer, at its most profound level, helps us see God in and through our struggles. The Prayer encourages us to stop attempting to reject or distance ourselves from our struggles so that we may learn to welcome and embrace them as a pathway to draw closer to God. When we welcome and embrace our struggles, we don't stop fighting. On the contrary, by welcoming and embracing our struggles, we are taking our surrender to God to the next level, which enables us to draw even greater strength from him.

There is a divine law at work here:

> *The more we struggle, the greater our need to surrender. The more we surrender, the closer to God we become. The closer to God we become, the more we are filled with his love, mercy, acceptance, grace and power to overcome our struggles.*

closing prayer

Recognize that you are a child of God and that he loves you unconditionally. Take a moment to become aware of your emotions, thoughts and how you are feeling physically before reciting the following prayer.

Welcome, welcome, welcome.
I welcome everything that comes to me in this moment
because I know it is for my healing.
I welcome all thoughts, feelings, emotions,
persons, situations and conditions.

I let go of my desire for security.
I let go of my desire for approval.
I let go of my desire for control.

I let go of my desire to change any
situation, condition,
person or myself.

I open myself to the
love and presence of God
and
His healing action and grace within.
Amen.

Mary Mrozowski 1925–1993

chapter 21

AN UNOFFICIAL STEP FOUR: THE SURRENDER PRAYER GROUP

We are not islands unto ourselves. We were not created to make it on our own. We are social beings that require healthy relationships for our physical, mental, emotional, and spiritual well-being and growth.

This book has presented the Surrender Prayer as an individual practice, but the Surrender Prayer has a corporate application as well. We believe that something glorious occurs when at least two people meet in prayer together with God as their foundation:

> *"For where two or three gather in my name, there am I with them."*
>
> **Matthew 18:20 (*NIV*)**

We may begin our journey with the Surrender Prayer as an individual practice, but we may soon feel drawn to practice the Prayer with others. As we use the Surrender Prayer to draw closer to God, we should seek to draw closer to people who are also striving to draw closer to God. Consequently, when we feel *safely* led to do so, we may begin practicing the Prayer with fellow practitioners who can understand and empathize with our struggles.

> *Two are better than one, because they have a good reward for their toil. For if they fall, one will lift up his fellow. But woe to him who is alone when he falls and has not another to lift him up! Again, if two lie together, they keep warm, but how can one keep warm alone? And though a man might prevail against one who is alone, two will withstand him—a threefold cord is not quickly broken.*
>
> **Ecclesiastes 4:9–12 (*ESV*)**

(See also Proverbs 27:17.)

Some of us may fear praying with others because group prayer requires a certain level of emotional intimacy and vulnerability. We may fear opening up to another person because of past hurts. Many of us have trusted others and have been betrayed. And many of us have been trusted by others and have betrayed such trust. Unfortunately, sooner or later, we all experience some level of disappointment and hurt in every meaningful relationship. As imperfect beings, we are incapable of creating perfect relationships.

* **List the relationships that you have with people (now or in the past), which have been most painful to you? What has been the cause of such pain?**

_____

_____

_____

_____

_____

* **In what ways do you escape life by isolating yourself from others? Why do you do these things?**

_____

_____

_____

_____

_____

* **What makes you feel most lonely? Why?**

_____

_____

_____

_____

_____

When we practice the Surrender Prayer, we learn to accept our imperfections just as we learn to accept the imperfections of others. But our acceptance of each other's imperfections does not require us to throw caution to the wind. Our personal safety comes first in our group Prayer practice just as it does within our individual Prayer practice. As such, we should only begin practicing the Surrender Prayer with those who understand and agree with the rules, principles, safeguards and boundaries of Surrender Prayer group practice.

We have provided instructions for a Surrender Prayer group on page 201. The format for the Surrender Prayer group is based on what we believe to be seven essential elements of Christian fellowship. The importance of fellowship cannot be overstated. Without the love, support and acceptance of others surrounding us, our spiritual development and advancement will at best come to a standstill, and, at worst, begin to regress.

mutual acceptance

The first essential element of the Surrender Prayer group is mutual acceptance. Please remember that acceptance is neither the approval of our own personal struggles, nor the approval of another's, but the decision to accept and love others and ourselves as we all seek to overcome our struggles by surrendering them to God.

> *Therefore, accept one another, just as Christ also accepted us to the glory of God.*
>
> **Romans 15:7 (*NASB*)**

Consequently, we all need to be a part of a fellowship of believers who will accept and empathize with our wounds, weaknesses, failures, and sins. We should search for and find others who will not intentionally reject, judge, condemn, criticize, hurt, manipulate or offend us on account of our struggles.

> *You, therefore, have no excuse, you who pass judgment on someone else, for at whatever point you judge another, you are condemning yourself, because you who pass judgment do the same things.*
>
> **Romans 2:1 (*NIV*)**

All members of the Surrender Prayer group should know that they can share whatever is on their hearts and minds without fear of being ostracized, rejected, criticized, excluded, or looked down upon. We all need a place where we can authentically express our struggles and weaknesses: a place where we can be real and honest with ourselves and with each other.

We Christians should strive to imitate the unconditional acceptance that we receive from God by unconditionally accepting each other within our Surrender Prayer Group so that the feelings of shame, guilt and embarrassment, which hinder our recovery, may be overcome by the love of God. The Surrender Prayer group should be a place where all individuals—no matter what sin or issue they are dealing with—will feel welcomed, accepted and loved by the group.

> *"Do not judge, or you too will be judged. For in the same way you judge others, you will be judged, and with the measure you use, it will be measured to you.*
>
> *"Why do you look at the speck of sawdust in your brother's eye and pay no attention to the plank in your own eye? How can you say to your brother, 'Let me take the speck out of your eye,' when all the time there is a plank in your own eye? You hypocrite, first take the plank out of your own eye, and then you will see clearly to remove the speck from your brother's eye."*
>
> **Matthew 7:1–5 (*NIV*)**

> *There is only one Lawgiver and Judge, the one who is able to save and destroy. But you—who are you to judge your neighbor?*
>
> **James 4:12 (*NIV*)**

(See also Luke 6:31, 37–38, 42; Matthew 7:3–4; and Romans 12:3.)

* **How have you been rejected, judged or looked down upon by others inside and outside of the church? What effect did these negative experiences have on you?**

_____

_____

_____

_____

_____

_____

Within the Surrender Prayer group, there is no place for division, discrimination, biases, or prejudice based upon race, ethnicity, socioeconomic class, political affiliation, sexual orientation, sex, gender, gender role, or Christian denomination. Debates and arguments about Christian theology, Biblical interpretation, Biblical infallibility and inerrancy, and views on abortion and homosexuality, which have the potential to divide and disrupt the Surrender Prayer group, should be avoided.

> *Do not get involved in foolish discussions about spiritual pedigrees or in quarrels and fights about obedience to Jewish laws. These things are useless and a waste of time. If people are causing divisions among you, give a first and second warning. After that, have nothing more to do with them.*
>
> **Titus 3:9–10 (NLT)**

> *Remind everyone about these things, and command them in God's presence to stop fighting over words. Such arguments are useless, and they can ruin those who hear them.*
>
> **2 Timothy 2:14 (NLT)**

> *Therefore let us stop passing judgment on one another. Instead, make up your mind not to put any stumbling block or obstacle in the way of a brother or sister.*
>
> **Romans 14:13 (NIV)**

(See also Colossians 3:11 and Galatians 3:28.)

The Surrender Prayer group should not be a platform for the delivery of our personal views on such issues, but a community for each of us to give and to receive the love and acceptance that we need to support and facilitate our drawing nearer to God and our transformation into the likeness of his Son. Of course, individual members may join other communities and organizations (whose views mirror their own) in order to advocate for such causes and to discuss matters that often lead to division, but the main purpose of the Surrender Prayer group is to accept and support each other as we all seek to overcome our struggles by accessing the power of God through surrender.

> *As for the one who is weak in faith, welcome him, but not to quarrel over opinions. One person believes he may eat anything, while the weak person eats only vegetables. Let not the one who eats despise the one who abstains, and let not the one who abstains pass judgment on the one who eats, for God has welcomed him. Who are you to pass judgment on the servant of another? It is before his own master that he stands or falls. And he will be upheld, for the Lord is able to make him stand.*
>
> **Romans 14:1–4 (*ESV*)**

> *And we urge you, brothers and sisters, warn those who are idle and disruptive, encourage the disheartened, help the weak, be patient with everyone.*
>
> **1 Thessalonians 5:14 (*NIV*)**

> *You, then, why do you judge your brother or sister? Or why do you treat them with contempt? For we will all stand before God's judgment seat.*
>
> **Romans 14:10 (*NIV*)**

Accordingly, we value the unity of the Surrender Prayer group over the particular personal viewpoints and opinions of individual group members. No controversy, difference of opinion, demagoguery, or proselytizing should ever threaten to overshadow the primary goals of the Surrender Prayer group. Your group is designed to help you overcome your struggles and to draw closer to God. Therefore, group members should be accepting of each other's various perspectives, outlooks and worldviews. Unity—not division—is vital:

> *I appeal to you, brothers and sisters, in the name of our Lord Jesus Christ, that all of you agree with one another in what you say and that there be no divisions among you, but that you be perfectly united in mind and thought. My brothers and sisters, some from Chloe's household have informed me that there are quarrels among you. What I mean is this: One of you says, "I follow Paul"; another, "I follow Apollos"; another, "I follow Cephas"; still another, "I follow Christ."*
>
> *Is Christ divided? Was Paul crucified for you? Were you baptized in the name of Paul?*
>
> **1 Corinthians 1:10–13 (*NIV*)**

> *Be completely humble and gentle; be patient, bearing with one another in love.*
>
> **Ephesians 4:2 (*NIV*)**

mutual confession

The second essential element of the Surrender Prayer group is mutual confession. Mutual confession necessitates a give and take; it is a two-way street. Mutual confession requires us to share our own personal failures, weaknesses, experiences, struggles, hopes and triumphs with our group; and also requires everyone within our group to share their own personal failures, weaknesses, experiences, struggles, hopes and triumphs with us.

We all fail; we all struggle; and we all need God to empower us to overcome our weaknesses. The Surrender Prayer group is about being real with one another. We should all belong to a community where we feel safe enough to put down our fronts and façades. We all need to belong to a community where we can share our struggles with each other so that acceptance, encouragement, healing, mutual support and spiritual growth can take place.

* **Which of your struggles cause you to feel fear, shame or embarrassment when you think of sharing your story with another person?**

_____

_____

_____

_____

_____

_____

_____

_____

When confession is mutual, it becomes far more difficult to cast a judgmental glance at the weaknesses of others because our failures and weaknesses are on display as well. Through mutual confession, we learn to understand and empathize with the weaknesses of others, just as others learn to understand and empathize with our own weaknesses. We take the risk of revealing our souls to others, and begin allowing them to shed love's light upon the darkest and most hidden parts of our own souls because we know that we are all taking the same risk of self-exposure together. Consequently, all members of your group should share their own personal struggles with each other.

> *Therefore confess your sins to each other and pray for each other so that you may be healed. The prayer of a righteous person is powerful and effective.*
>
> **James 5:16 (NIV)**

shared leadership

The third essential element of the Surrender Prayer group is shared leadership. Leadership responsibility should be distributed among all. Every group member should have access to, and meaningful input and involvement in the decision-making process of the group because each group member has something to add to the group. In other words, everyone has something to teach (and learn from) each other.

> *Let the message of Christ dwell among you richly as you teach and admonish one another with all wisdom through psalms, hymns, and songs from the Spirit, singing to God with gratitude in your hearts.*
>
> **Colossians 3:16 (NIV)**

There are no individual leaders per se in the group. As a result, before any definitive action is undertaken by the Surrender Prayer group as a whole, substantial unanimity should be achieved. In addition, any positions that are necessary to fulfill group needs should be filled and vacated strictly on a rotating basis.

> *"Don't let anyone call you 'Rabbi,' for you have only one teacher, and all of you are equal as brothers and sisters. And don't address anyone here on earth as 'Father,' for only God in heaven is your Father. And don't let anyone call you 'Teacher,' for you have only one teacher, the Messiah. The greatest among you must be a servant. But those who exalt themselves will be humbled, and those who humble themselves will be exalted."*
>
> **Matthew 23:8–12 (*NLT*)**

Within your Surrender Prayer group, leadership should at all times be practiced from a position of humility and weakness. At no time should any member ever feel unable to disclose and discuss their battles with temptation, sin, weakness, oppression, poverty, or any other struggle. In fact, an individual's willingness to disclose his or her struggles and weaknesses is the most important characteristic of leadership within the group.

To help all Surrender Prayer group members remain open with their weaknesses and struggles, no member should ever be placed on a pedestal. This stance makes it far more difficult for hidden sin to fester and grow within the community because individuals are never placed within any leadership position in which they are ever expected to be struggle-free. All members should be able to share their struggles within the community no matter what those issues are. We are all weak. Therefore, we should all lead with our weakness in the group to ensure that God's Spirit continually empowers us to overcome our sins and struggles.

corporate prayer

The fourth essential element of the Surrender Prayer group is corporate prayer for the needs of fellow group members. Please note that this prayer is separate and distinct from the group practice of Surrender Prayer. Accordingly, each Surrender Prayer group meeting should include an assigned portion of time for individual group members to pray for the needs of each other.

> *They all joined together constantly in prayer, along with the women and Mary the mother of Jesus, and with his brothers.*
>
> **Acts 1:14 (*NIV*)**

> *They devoted themselves to the apostles' teaching and to fellowship, to the breaking of bread and to prayer.*
>
> **Acts 2:42 (*NIV*)**

> *Therefore confess your sins to each other and pray for each other so that you may be healed. The prayer of a righteous person is powerful and effective.*
>
> **James 5:16 (*NIV*)**

forgiveness

The fifth essential element of the Surrender Prayer group is forgiveness. When we are hurt by someone in our group, we should strive to forgive.

> *Therefore, as God's chosen people, holy and dearly loved, clothe yourselves with compassion, kindness, humility, gentleness and patience. Bear with each other and forgive one another if any of you has a grievance against someone. Forgive as the Lord forgave you. And over all these virtues put on love, which binds them all together in perfect unity.*
>
> **Colossians 3:12–14 (*NIV*)**

> *Be kind and compassionate to one another, forgiving each other, just as in Christ God forgave you.*
>
> **Ephesians 4:32 (*NIV*)**

> *Do not repay anyone evil for evil. Be careful to do what is right in the eyes of everyone. If it is possible, as far as it depends on you, live at peace with everyone.*
>
> **Romans 12:17–18 (*NIV*)**

* **Which hurts are you not ready to get over, forgive, heal, or recover from?**

_____

_____

_____

_____

_____

_____

_____

_____

* **What is holding you back from moving forward and letting go?**

_____

_____

_____

_____

_____

_____

* **Does it hurt more to hold onto the hurt or to let it go?**

_____

_____

_____

_____

_____

_____

And when we have hurt another in our group, we should seek to make amends with such person.

> *"Therefore, if you are offering your gift at the altar and there remember that your brother or sister has something against you, leave your gift there in front of the altar. First go and be reconciled to them; then come and offer your gift."*
>
> **Matthew 5:23–24 (*NIV*)**

mutual support

The sixth essential element of Surrender Prayer group is mutual support. We choose to be in the Surrender Prayer group to receive support from others when we are in need, and to provide support to others when they are in need.

> *And let us consider how we may spur one another on toward love and good deeds, not giving up meeting together, as some are in the habit of doing, but encouraging one another—and all the more as you see the Day approaching.*
>
> **Hebrews 10:24–25 (*NIV*)**

> *So if there is any encouragement in Christ, any comfort from love, any participation in the Spirit, any affection and sympathy, complete my joy by being of the same mind, having the same love, being in full accord and of one mind. Do nothing from rivalry or conceit, but in humility count others more significant than yourselves. Let each of you look not only to his own interests, but also to the interests of others. Have this mind among yourselves, which is yours in Christ Jesus.*
>
> **Philippians 2:1–5 (ESV)**

> *Bear one another's burdens, and thereby fulfill the law of Christ.*
>
> **Galatians 6:2 (NASB)**

(See also Acts 2:44–47, 4:32–35; Romans 1:12; and 1 Thessalonians 5:11.)

* **How has your pride or fear prevented you from asking for the help you need to overcome your struggles?**

_____

_____

_____

_____

_____

_____

_____

_____

_____

* List examples in your life when you have not asked for help (or put off asking for help for too long) when you really needed it.

_____

_____

_____

_____

_____

_____

_____

_____

* Why did you delay asking for the help?

_____

_____

_____

_____

commitment to mercy and justice

The seventh and final essential element of the Surrender Prayer group is caring for the poor and seeking justice for the oppressed.

> "Then the King will say to those on his right, 'Come, you who are blessed by my Father; take your inheritance, the kingdom prepared for you since the creation of the world. For I was hungry and you gave me something to eat, I was thirsty and you gave me something to drink, I was a stranger and you invited me in, I needed clothes and you clothed me, I was sick and you looked after me, I was in prison and you came to visit me.'
>
> "Then the righteous will answer him, 'Lord, when did we see you hungry and feed you, or thirsty and give you something to drink? When did we see you a stranger and invite you in, or needing clothes and clothe you? When did we see you sick or in prison and go to visit you?'
>
> "The King will reply, 'Truly I tell you, whatever you did for one of the least of these brothers and sisters of mine, you did for me.'"
>
> **Matthew 25:34–40 (NIV)**

> *Speak up for those who cannot speak for themselves;*
> *ensure justice for those being crushed. Yes, speak up*
> *for the poor and helpless, and see that they get justice.*
>
> **Proverbs 31:8 (*NLT*)**

(See also Isaiah 1:17, 58:6–11; Acts 20:35; and Luke 4:16–21.)

We who practice the Surrender Prayer believe that our continued sobriety, healing, recovery, and connection to God are all spiritually linked to our commitment to mercy and justice. 12-Step Program members believe that: "We can only keep what we have by giving it away." The "it" they are talking about is our sobriety, healing, recovery, and connection with God. This belief is a derivative of the spiritual law that Jesus first introduced two thousand years ago: "It is more blessed to give than to receive" (Acts 20:35, NIV). In other words:

> *"Give, and you will receive. Your gift will return to*
> *you in full—pressed down, shaken together to make*
> *room for more, running over, and poured into your*
> *lap. The amount you give will determine the amount*
> *you get back."*
>
> **Luke 6:38 (*NLT*)**

Consequently, we Christians should give of ourselves, and care for our brothers and sisters in need (both locally and globally) by contributing our human, social, and financial capital as we are individually and collectively called to do so by God. Please ask God to show you how to begin providing for those in need. To fulfill this spiritual responsibility, one may choose to contribute to a reputable charitable organization that provides for the basic human needs of the poor or advocates for the oppressed.

Please note that the definition of the poor and the oppressed also includes the poor in spirit and those suffering from addiction, depression, or any other mental, emotional or physical health issue. Therefore, we may fulfill this group element by sharing how the Surrender Prayer has helped free us from the oppression of our own spiritual strongholds when doing so may assist others in obtaining their own spiritual freedom.

closing prayer

Dear God, if it be your will, I pray that you lead me to join—or start—a Surrender Prayer group where I and other group members will be accepted regardless of our sins, weaknesses and failures. If it be your will, lead me to a community of safety and trust where I can unashamedly share my struggles, and hear the struggles of my brothers and sisters in Christ without judging or being judged by others. Lord, direct me to a group where no man or woman is designated as the leader, but where your Holy Spirit dwells and guides in the substantial unanimity of the community. Let the group be a place where prayer is cherished and undertaken for the benefit of both myself and for all my brothers and sisters in Christ. I pray that you place me within a group of believers where humility, forgiveness, mutual support and love are not just talked about—but practiced. Lastly, Lord, you said that it is more blessed to give than to receive. For that reason, please place in my heart the desire to care for the poor and to seek justice for the oppressed in accordance with your will for me. Amen!

CONCLUSION

As you progress in your prayer practice, it is extremely important that you always remain kind and patient with yourself. As stated previously, the Surrender Prayer is neither a contest nor a competition with ourselves or with others. Our walk with God is not a sprint toward a finish line: we are seeking God daily to help us overcome our struggles. Personal judgments, self-criticism, and comparisons with others have no place within the Surrender Prayer practice. Your Prayer should provide you with an established place of trust, safety, unconditional love, acceptance, and non-judgment for it to be effective. We are all works in progress. So please remember that our progression is in accordance with God's timetable—not our own.

Just as there is no right or wrong way to pray, there is also no right or wrong way to practice the Surrender Prayer. This book has provided you with simple guidelines to help you along your own individual path. Your personal practice will allow you to determine what is effective and what is not. It is your responsibility to make what has been written in this book your own by keeping what works for you, discarding what doesn't, and adding whatever the Spirit directs you to add.

What you have read is my best attempt at making sense of this world and my existence in it. It is a distillation of what has sustained me through my trials; and is the lens through which I view the pain, suffering and injustice that I both experience in my life and perceive in the lives of others. To the best of my limited ability, it represents the keys to surviving your own personal trials and tribulations, but also represents an opportunity for you to begin thriving spiritually—no matter what your current circumstances.

> *I am not saying this because I am in need, for I have learned to be content whatever the circumstances. I know what it is to be in need, and I know what it is to have plenty. I have learned the secret of being content in any and every situation, whether well fed or hungry, whether living in plenty or in want. I can do all this through him who gives me strength.*
>
> **Philippians 4:11–13 (NIV)**

You will find God in your struggles, and after you find him, you will realize that he has been waiting there for you all along. He has always been there in the pain and in the struggle with you. The Surrender Prayer will help you discover his presence, and begin to make sense of the connection between God's love and your struggles.

The turning point for me was the revelation that I had nothing to prove to God, which meant that I no longer had anything to hide from him. This revelation began with me seeing that too much of my life had been consumed with feelings of inadequacy, fear, self-hate, envy, loneliness, rejection, worthlessness, disappointment and failure. Those feelings led to self-isolation, self-sabotage, addiction, debilitating procrastination, damaged relationships, and an unbridled, rationalized, self-justified selfishness.

I began the life-long process of allowing God to begin healing my self-destructive feelings and behaviors when I stopped blaming those who had hurt me deeply for the negative circumstances of my life. Even if others really were to blame for many of my problems, I realized that continuing to blame them for my failures, weaknesses and inadequacies would never provide me with the means to rise above the struggles that engulfed me. I realized that continuing to blame others for my circumstances would only allow me to continue giving myself excuses for not ever living my life to its fullest potential. In other words, blaming others for never getting better or doing better was no longer good enough for me. I wanted more than that for myself.

During this period, my job as a social worker provided me with the opportunity to work with many amazing individuals who—even though, they had been through far worse life experiences than I had—didn't make excuses for themselves. God used these wonderful people to help me break through my personal wall of denial so that I could begin seeing myself as I truly was: a man in desperate need of God to accept and love him for *everything* that he is.

It was at this point of self-discovery that God stepped in during a time of daily morning prayer. I felt his presence. His Spirit spoke to mine. And he told me that he loved me just as I was. He told me that he had always loved me and that he would always love me. He said that there was nothing that I had ever done or would ever do that could stop him from loving me. He told me that everything about myself that made me feel ashamed never made him ashamed of me. My God told me not to believe all the voices inside (and outside of) my head that told me I would never be good enough. He told me that I didn't have to prove myself to him or to anybody else. And he told me that he would never, ever leave, abandon, neglect, or reject me.

I broke down in tears that morning…and I strive to remember his words of love whenever I fall back into my old, self-destructive ways of feeling, thinking, and acting.

The good news we Christians believe is that God loves us just as we are, which is the foundation of the Surrender Prayer. God's love is both unconditional and unlimited. Everything that you believe makes you ugly, unworthy, and unlovable, God views as part of his precise creation.

> *For you created my inmost being; you knit me together in my mother's womb. I praise you because I am fearfully and wonderfully made; your works are wonderful, I know that full well. My frame was not hidden from you when I was made in the secret place, when I was woven together in the depths of the earth. Your eyes saw my unformed body; all the days ordained for me were written in your book before one of them came to be.*
>
> **Psalm 139:13–16 (*NIV*)**

Please remember that God is incapable of making mistakes—all of us are part of his very good creation. (Genesis 1:31) This means that our scars, weaknesses, struggles, sins, and humiliations have never resulted in God rejecting us.

> *Hear my voice when I call, Lord; be merciful to me and answer me. My heart says of you, "Seek his face!" Your face, Lord, I will seek. Do not hide your face from me, do not turn your servant away in anger; you have been my helper. Do not reject me or forsake me, God my Savior. Though my father and mother forsake me, the Lord will receive me.*
>
> **Psalm 27:7–10 (*NIV*)**

Instead, they represent an opportunity for us to draw nearer to him in order to experience his grace, love and healing. So let us begin the process of surrendering the things to God that have kept us captive for too long.

Therefore, since we are surrounded by such a great cloud of witnesses, let us throw off everything that hinders and the sin that so easily entangles. And let us run with perseverance the race marked out for us, fixing our eyes on Jesus, the pioneer and perfecter of faith. For the joy set before him he endured the cross, scorning its shame, and sat down at the right hand of the throne of God. Consider him who endured such opposition from sinners, so that you will not grow weary and lose heart.

Hebrews 12:1–3 (*NIV*)

Finally, as you embark upon this new journey, please remember that there is hope; you are loved; and that accessing the power of Jesus Christ is, always has been, and always will be the answer to all of your troubles.

For I can do everything through Christ, who gives me strength.

Philippians 4:13 (*NLT*)

Amen.

THE SURRENDER PRAYER SUMMARY GUIDE

Identify my anchor: _____.

As I begin the Surrender Prayer, I acknowledge that I am anchored in God's love and protection.

STEP 1: *awareness*
(approximately 3 minutes)
With a willingness to face my struggle, I:
- Identify my struggle.
- Present my struggle to God.

STEP 2: *acceptance*
(approximately 5 minutes)
With a willingness to accept what is, I:
- Resist battling my struggle with my own strength.
- Sit with my struggle.

STEP 3: *surrender*
(approximately 7 minutes)
With a willingness to trust God, I:
- Invite God into my struggle and allow God to fight it for me.
- Wait patiently in stillness, silence and solitude for God to strengthen me.

As I complete the Surrender Prayer, I remain anchored in God's love and protection.

THE SURRENDER PRAYER FULL INSTRUCTIONS

Before beginning the Surrender Prayer, please:

(1) Choose your spiritual anchor (see p. 68) to ground and center yourself in God. When confronting your struggle, your anchor represents your faith and hope that your God is always there to protect you, unconditionally love you and keep you safe—no matter what. Your anchor may be as short as one word, or as long as a few words. Examples include: "Jesus"; "Help"; "Love"; "God"; "Save me"; "Help me"; "Love me"; "Protect me"; and "The Lord is my strength and shield." Whenever you feel distracted or overwhelmed by your feelings, thoughts, or memories, gently return to your anchor to help ground, or center, yourself within God's protection. When grounding yourself in God's love and protection, please believe in faith that Jesus is holding you safely in his arms as you face your struggle.

(2) Set aside at least 15 minutes of your day when you will not be interrupted or distracted. As your practice progresses, feel free to lengthen your time of prayer.

(3) Go alone to your "closet" (Matthew 6:6), a quiet place where you can pray alone and undisturbed for the next 15 minutes.

(4) Sit in a comfortable chair or couch that provides sufficient support for your back.

(5) Remember who your God is:

- God loves you unconditionally.
- God accepts you for all that you are.
- God will never reject you.
- God will never leave you or abandon you.
- God is right there with you in your struggle.
- God feels and experiences all of the pain, sorrow, grief, shame, guilt, embarrassment, anger, resentment, temptation, doubt, and fear that you feel and experience.
- God is waiting for you to surrender your struggle to him.
- God will ultimately strengthen you to overcome your struggles.

> *No power in the sky above or in the earth below— indeed, nothing in all creation will ever be able to separate us from the love of God that is revealed in Christ Jesus our Lord.*
>
> **Romans 8:39 (NLT)**

> *What shall we say about such wonderful things as these? If God is for us, who can ever be against us?*
>
> **Romans 8:31 (NLT)**

(6) Set a timer for 15 minutes.

(7) Lastly, if you feel safe doing so, close your eyes.

[If you ever feel unsafe at anytime during the Prayer, simply: (1) open your eyes; (2) stop the Prayer; (3) go back and review who your God is; and (4) take a break for the day, or for as long as you need, before deciding if you should continue the Prayer.

Be kind and patient with yourself. This is not a contest, competition or race. Personal judgments, self-criticism, and comparisons with others have no place in this Prayer or in any other prayer. For the Surrender Prayer to be effective, it should provide you with an established place of trust, safety, unconditional love, acceptance, and non-judgment.]

STEP 1: *awareness*

(approximately 3 minutes)

> *"For all that is secret will eventually be brought into the open, and everything that is concealed will be brought to light and made known to all."*
>
> **Luke 8:17 (NLT)**

With a willingness to face my struggle, I:
- Identify my struggle.
- Present my struggle to God.

Bring your struggle to God. Your struggle is any conflict, wound, or sin that causes you pain and distress. Your struggle is what you believe makes you feel rejected, weak, unworthy, guilty, unlovable, or anxious. In most cases, your struggle will be a specific problem or issue (examples include: depression, trauma, addiction, shame, uncontrollable anger, or any form of discrimination).

STEP 2: *acceptance*

(approximately 5 minutes)

> *The Lord is my light and my salvation—whom shall I fear? The Lord is the strength of my life—of whom shall I be afraid?*
>
> **Psalm 27:1 (NIV)**

With a willingness to accept what is, I:
- Resist battling my struggle with my own strength.
- Sit with my struggle.

Admit to God that you are powerless to overcome your struggles without him. To the best of your ability, stop fighting, resisting, and battling in your own strength.

Be still, sit and face your struggle and any distractions that may arise. As your thoughts, feelings, memories, experiences, and any distractions come to mind, gently acknowledge and accept their presence—no matter what they are. Do not judge or condemn yourself for anything that you perceive, think, or feel. Mindfully observe your struggle and any resultant distractions in the present moment without attempting to escape them. Remember that God will never reject, judge, or stop loving you because of your struggles—no matter what they are. Keep your struggle in God's loving presence—don't allow it to retreat back into the shadows.

Ground yourself in God's love and protection with your spiritual anchor. When confronting your struggle, your anchor represents your faith and hope that your God is always there to protect you, unconditionally love you and keep you safe—no matter what. Your anchor may be as short as one word, or as long as a few words. Examples include: "Jesus," "Help," "Love," "God," "Save me," "Help me," "Love me" and "The Lord is my strength and shield." Whenever you feel distracted or overwhelmed by your feelings or thoughts, gently return to your anchor to help center yourself within God's protection. When grounding yourself in God's love and protection, please believe in faith that Jesus is holding you safely in his arms as you face your struggle.

STEP 3: *surrender*

(approximately 7 minutes)

> But Moses told the people, *"Don't be afraid. Just stand still and watch the LORD rescue you today. The Egyptians you see today will never be seen again."*
>
> **Exodus 14:13 *(NLT)***

With a willingness to trust God, I:
- Invite God into my struggle and allow God to fight it for me.
- Wait patiently in stillness, silence and solitude for God to strengthen me.

Hand over your struggle to God. Give your burdens to him. Believe in faith that he is there to take them from you. Surrender it all to him. Ask God to fight those feelings, thoughts, experiences, memories, behaviors and compulsions that have led you to do things that you no longer want to do. Step aside to allow room for God to step in.

Gradually remove your personal strength, opposition and resistance from your struggle while intentionally drawing God's strength into the struggle. Stop using your own limited resources to fight for yourself, and begin tapping into the unlimited power reserves of your Higher Power to fight for you. Pull God into your struggle by demanding that he arise, and come to your rescue. Imagine and believe in faith that: (1) God is there with you in the struggle; (2) that God understands, accepts and experiences all that you feel, think and suffer in your struggle; and (3) that God is (and always will be) fighting your battle for you.

Believe that Jesus is holding you and loving you through your sadness, sin, weakness, failures, wounds, hurts, trauma, depression, despair, anger, regret, lust, loneliness, oppression, injustice, abandonment, poverty, confusion, anxiety or pain. Believe that Jesus is partnering with you, and that he will help you carry and overcome your burdens. Have faith that God accepts and loves you unconditionally in your struggles—that he will never reject, abandon, condemn, judge, or stop loving you.

Continue to hold onto your spiritual anchor, and ground yourself within the unconditional love and security of God while you wait in stillness, silence and solitude for God to strengthen and empower you to overcome your struggles. Remember that your spiritual anchor represents your faith and hope that God is always there to protect you, love you and keep you safe—no matter what you experience while confronting your struggles. Center yourself within God's protection, and wait patiently until you feel God take up your battle and lighten your load. Your prayer has ended when you have entered God's resting place.

Our situations and circumstances may not change. Our battles and conflicts may still remain. But we now have the tools to help us endure, resist and overcome our struggles. We can now develop the ability to turn to God—instead of turning to our destructive coping mechanisms and self-medicating behaviors—to help us find peace, relief, and rest from our pain.

Thank you, Jesus. Amen.

Lord, how many are my foes! How many rise up against me! Many are saying of me, "God will not deliver him." But you, Lord, are a shield around me, my glory, the One who lifts my head high. I call out to the Lord, and he answers me from his holy mountain. I lie down and sleep; I wake again, because the Lord sustains me. I will not fear though tens of thousands assail me on every side. Arise, Lord! Deliver me, my God! Strike all my enemies on the jaw; break the teeth of the wicked. From the Lord comes deliverance. May your blessing be on your people.

Psalm 3 (NIV)

SURRENDER PRAYER GROUP

We have provided the following Surrender Prayer group structure as a suggested format for meetings. Please modify it as necessary to meet the needs of your particular group. The group may initially be as small as two people, but should probably grow to no larger than 12 adults to ensure that there is sufficient time for everyone to speak and share prayer requests. The group may take place in a space provided by a church, or in a room of a building that rents space for meetings or classes. For safety reasons, it is recommended that the group take place in a member's home only if the homeowner knows all group members. Finally, the group should take place on a day and time that allows its members to consistently attend without difficulty.

GROUND RULES

(1) Please keep sharing focused on your own personal experience, thoughts, and feelings. Begin sentences with "I" (not "You"). Encourage comfort and support by sharing your own needs and experiences.

(2) Please limit the time to three to five minutes per share. Kindly limit your own talking to allow others to share. Please allow equal time for everyone in the group to say what is on their hearts.

(3) Avoid topics that can lead to dissension or distraction. Also avoid provocative or abusive language. The emphasis should be on honesty, recovery, and healing. If someone feels that another person's remarks are too explicit, they may so signify by quietly raising their hand. Offensive language should be avoided at all times.

(4) There is no crosstalk. Crosstalk is when two or more individuals engage in conversation, excluding the rest of the group. Each person is free to express his or her feelings without interruption. Please keep your comments brief, take turns talking, and don't interrupt others. Please respect each other's rights to self-expression without comment.

(5) We are here to support one another, not fix one another. No advice giving please. Please do not probe or judge others. Accept what others say without comment, realizing it is true for them. Assume responsibility only for your own feelings, thoughts, and actions.

(6) Refrain from criticizing or defending others. Lovingly hold others accountable for their behavior only if they ask you to do so. Otherwise, recognize that we are all accountable to Christ, and it is not our place to defend or criticize others.

(7) Confidentiality is a basic requirement. What is shared in the group stays in the group to ensure safety and openness. The only exception would be if one person threatens to injure him or herself, or others. Please keep the name, address, and phone number of anyone you meet or learn about in this meeting to yourself.

GROUP FORMAT

It is very helpful to select a person with an established Surrender Prayer practice to facilitate the group, but this is not a requirement. Some groups rotate facilitators frequently while others may choose to elect a person with more experience in the prayer to facilitate the group for an extended period of time.

This presented format is optional and should be tailored to suit the needs of the group. The most important element is the time spent together in fellowship.

(1) Open with an established, short, written prayer or Bible verse that will be used to begin each Surrender Prayer group. The following prayer and Bible verse have been provided as examples:

Today, right now in this very moment, we surrender our battles to you. We admit that we don't have the power to overcome our struggles. Please give us the faith to believe that we can stop fighting so that you can start fighting for us. Please come to our aid in our time of need. Don't delay! Rise up, God, and answer our call to you! Draw near to us as we draw near to you. Give us the power to overcome our struggles. Give us the power to choose you instead of the destructive addictions, habits, obsessions and compulsions that we have used to survive our pain. Reveal your will for our lives, and give us the strength to fulfill the purpose for which we were born just as our Lord and Savior Jesus Christ fulfilled his ultimate purpose. Teach us how to enter your rest. And show us that you will always be our strength, refuge and ever-present help in our time of trouble. Amen!

> *I lift up my eyes to the mountains—where does my help come from? My help comes from the Lord, the Maker of heaven and earth. He will not let your foot slip—he who watches over you will not slumber; indeed, he who watches over Israel will neither slumber nor sleep. The Lord watches over you—the Lord is your shade at your right hand; the sun will not harm you by day, nor the moon by night. The Lord will keep you from all harm—he will watch over your life; the Lord will watch over your coming and going both now and forevermore.*
>
> **Psalm 121 (NIV)**

(2) Go around the circle, and ask everyone to briefly introduce themselves to the group.

(3) Read the group ground rules.

(4) Surrender Prayer periods are usually 15-20 minutes. They begin with 3 rings of a pleasant gong or bell, a short reading of a psalm, poem or prayer, followed by one more gong or bell to start the prayer period.

(5) End the prayer period with three rings of the gong. The group facilitator may then recite a short prayer like the Our Father/The Lord's Prayer.

(6) The group facilitator next reads the chosen reading for the day, which has been pre-approved by the group conscience. The reading may be from The Surrender Prayer book or from another appropriate and relevant source.

(7) There is usually 20 minutes of individual sharing about the reading, the practice of Surrender Prayer, or whatever else may be on the hearts and minds of group members.

(8) Provide an opportunity for all group members to present prayer requests for corporate prayer.

(9) End the group after an hour unless the group decides, beforehand, to establish a longer meeting time.

SAMPLE SURRENDER PRAYER GROUP MEETING

"We welcome you to this Surrender Prayer group, my name is _____ _____ and I will be leading us this month.

First, a reminder to please turn your phones off or to silent mode (rather than to vibrate) so that we do not experience any interruptions.

This group was formed to help each of us sustain, support, and enrich our own individual Surrender Prayer practice within a Christian community.

The only requirements for membership are a desire to: (1) establish the Surrender Prayer as a daily practice in your life, and (2) join and engage with a supportive fellowship of Christian believers.

Our prayer meeting is divided into four sections: a 15-minute Surrender Prayer period, a brief reading, a time of sharing, and a time for prayer requests.

The meeting begins promptly at ____ o'clock.

We encourage you to be on time; however, if you arrive late, please enter as quietly as possible.

May I have a volunteer to read the group guidelines?"

[(1) Select someone from the group to read the Group Guidelines.

(2) Read a short, written prayer that has been preselected by the group, which will be used to begin each Surrender Prayer group.

(3) Go around the circle and ask everyone to briefly introduce themselves, and state how long they've been attending this group meeting.

(4) Begin the Surrender Prayer with: (a) 3 rings of a pleasant gong or bell, (b) a short reading of a psalm, poem or prayer, and (c) one more gong or bell to start the actual Surrender Prayer period of 15-20 minutes.

(5) End the prayer period with three rings of the gong or bell. Provide a few quiet moments for everyone to come back to his or her surroundings. The group facilitator may then recite a short prayer like the Our Father.

(6) The group facilitator next reads the chosen reading for the day, which has been pre-approved by the group. The reading may be from The Surrender Prayer book or from another appropriate and relevant source.

(7) At the completion of the reading, the group facilitator announces:]

"The meeting is now open for sharing."

[(8) There is usually 20 minutes of individual sharing about the reading, the practice of Surrender Prayer, or whatever else may be on the hearts and minds of the group participants.

(9) When the sharing period is completed, the facilitator passes the basket for donations.

(10) The facilitator states:]

"While there are no dues or fees, we are self-supporting through our own contributions. Please provide what you can. If you feel led to do so, two dollars is the suggested donation amount. We use our donations to _____ _____ (choose all applicable: cover the weekly use of this space, supply refreshments, or provide funds to a charitable foundation)."

[(11)While the basket is passed around, the facilitator asks the following:]

"Before concluding the meeting, we would like to provide some time for prayer requests. Does anyone have any prayer requests that they would like the group to pray for?"

[(12) While the donations are collected, volunteers should be selected by the facilitator to pray for the prayer requests. No members should pray for their own individual prayer requests.

(13) When all donations have been collected, group members should then proceed to pray for each other in accordance with the prayer requests.

(14) At the conclusion of the prayers, the group facilitator calls the meeting to a close.]

NOTES

ABOUT
THE AUTHOR

A native of Harlem, New York, Kristian spent the first years of his career as an attorney. His desire to live a fulfilling life in service to God led him to quit the legal profession and attend the Rutgers University School of Social Work where he received his Master's degree. With a focus on individual and group therapy, he has worked in both Christian and secular non-profit agencies in New Jersey. He works with adolescents, adults and families, and has developed a unique approach to helping his clients discover how to identify, face and heal their wounds by relying upon the transformative power of God's love and acceptance. Kristian is a graduate of Brown University, Fordham University School of Law and Rutgers University School of Social Work.

CPSIA information can be obtained
at www.ICGtesting.com
Printed in the USA
BVOW10s1551030617

485932BV00005B/8/P